Contents

Introduction

The assumption that pupils who succeed at the end of Year 9 continue this pathway of success and succeed again at the end of Year 11, then 12 and 13, is false. There isn't a cast-iron link between success at the end of one key stage and success at the next. Past performance doesn't guarantee future performance.

Some pupils make giant strides between fourteen and sixteen, or sixteen and eighteen, leaping up from modest results in Year 9, for example, to outstanding results in Year 11. Others go from great performance at fourteen to modest grades at the end of their GCSE courses.

Why is this? We used to think it was to do with intelligence. But having taught thousands of pupils, and spoken to hundreds of them about their studies, we couldn't find any specific intellectual weaknesses that meant poor performance at GCSE. We've spent years looking and never found them. When we interviewed successful pupils what we *did* find was that they had certain habits, routines, attitudes and approaches to study. We found it over and over again – the successful pupils who got the best grades weren't the cleverest, they were the ones who worked a certain way. It's your skills, systems and approaches to study that are the best predictor of academic success.

Our work suggests that pupils who are successful score highly in the following characteristics or qualities:

» ***VISION*** – they know what they want to achieve.

» ***EFFORT*** – they put in many hours of proactive independent study.

» ***SYSTEMS*** – they organise their learning resources and their time.

» ***PRACTICE*** – they practise and develop their skills.

» ***ATTITUDE*** – they respond constructively to setbacks.

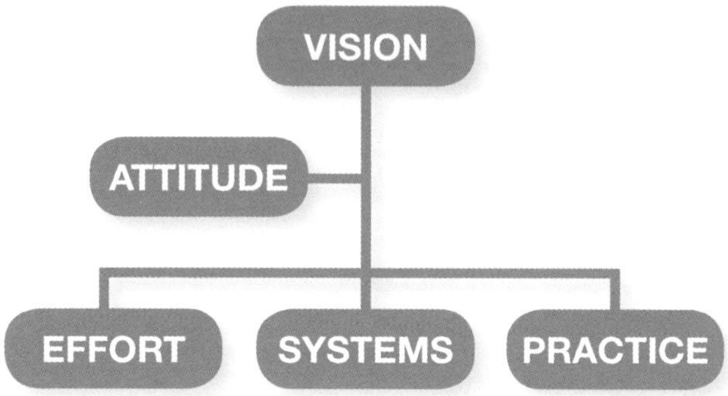

These characteristics beat intelligence hands down. Forget how clever you feel, or what set you're in – if you get to grips with what you want to achieve and why (V), you begin working harder (E), you organise your time and resources well (S), practise a certain way (P) and stay positive during setbacks (A), you're heading for great grades no matter what has happened to you up to now. Or, in other words:

Students who are success seekers are not bluffed by setback, poor performance, failure or academic adversity. They take the lesson to be learnt and move on. Martin (2010), p. 21

The VESPA Activities

The activities in this booklet are designed to:

» Raise awareness about the impact a quality/characteristic can have on your potential success.

» Encourage you to reflect on the strength of that quality on a personal level.

» Engage you in a task that develops you as a learner – a reflection, discussion, coaching conversation or experiment.

Each session is designed to take fifteen to twenty minutes to complete. We've included a variety of tasks under each heading, giving you a total of forty to start experimenting with.

Good luck!

September Activities

September can feel like a fresh start, a chance to try to be a better learner with new and effective habits. We certainly feel that way in September! The month can be what some people call an 'inflection point' or a turning point, a great opportunity to try something new. So this month's activities focus on aims and goals, and give you resources that will help clarify what it is you want to achieve. In short, you need to know *what success looks like for you*. That way, you can make good decisions as you work towards it.

1. Vision Activity: The Motivation Diamond

Sometimes, it's easier to express the motivations and desires that are important to us rather than the jobs or courses that might fulfil them. Professor Steven Reiss, who worked as a psychologist at Ohio State University, conducted studies with over 6,000 people to try to define their underlying motivations. He concluded his work by suggesting there are sixteen different motivations that guide all human behaviour. We've adjusted his list a little to make it more accessible and easy to work with. There are fifteen in ours.

Study the list below and decide which seem as though they might be most important to you. Once you've shortlisted nine of the fifteen, you then have to prioritise them using the diamond. At the top of the diamond, leading the others, should be the motivation that beats all others for you. Underneath, you can have two deputies alongside each other. Then come the rest.

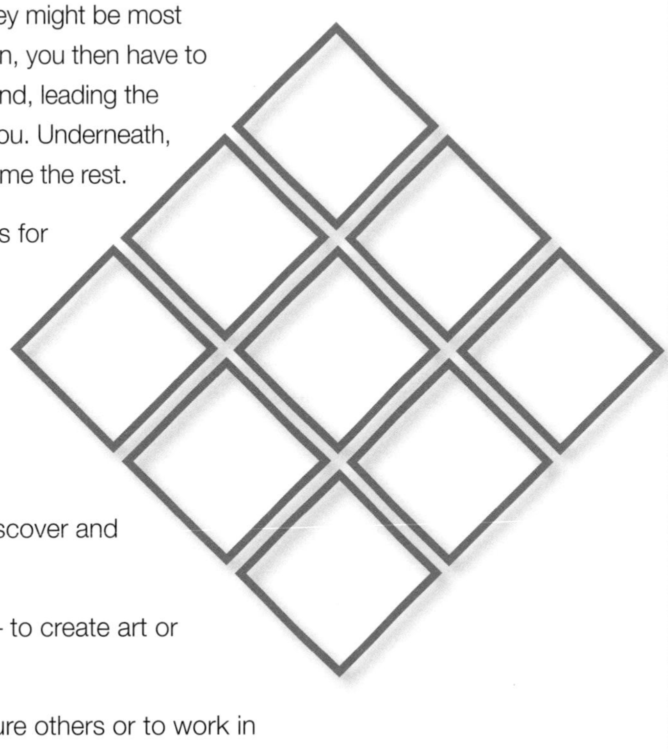

Fifteen possible motivations (adapted from Steven Reiss for the purposes of this task):

1. Acceptance: the need for approval, support and good feeling from those around you.
2. Competition: the need to pit yourself against others – to compete and win.
3. Curiosity: the need to learn, explore, research, discover and try new things.
4. Creativity: the need to design, write, draw, build – to create art or entertainment.
5. Family: the need to raise or help children, to nurture others or to work in small, loyal units supporting those around you.
6. Honour: the need to be loyal to the key values of a group or society – to observe the rules, do what is expected and guide others in these values.

7. Idealism: the need for fairness, equality and social justice.
8. Independence: the need for individuality – the ability to organise and run things your way.
9. Order: the need for organised, stable, predictable environments; creating routines and patterns.
10. Physical activity: the need for movement, exercise and physical challenge.
11. Power: the need for influence, the ability to determine the direction of others; the responsibility for the performance of groups.
12. Saving: the need to collect things, to own things and categorise or order them.
13. Social contact: the need for friends, to have extensive peer relationships.
14. Social status: the need to appear to be of a high social standing or a person of importance.
15. Tranquillity: the need to be calm, relaxed and safe.

Once you've drawn up your leading motivations, think about the times in your life when you are at your most energised. Times when you're buzzing with excitement, good feeling and happiness.

» What are you doing?

. . . .

. . . .

. . . .

» What elements of your motivation are being rewarded?

. . . .

. . . .

. . . .

Final Thoughts

The nature of our working lives are changing. People used to choose a profession or trade, and stick to it for the entirety of their working lives. Now, employment is much more fluid. The *Telegraph* recently summarised a study which showed people will, on average, work for six different employers and have between ten and twenty-five job interviews before they retire. 45% of us will be made redundant at least once. 46% of us will retrain completely and switch careers as we seek greater satisfaction.

So your experience will be different from that of your parents and teachers. Opportunities, careers and jobs will emerge that didn't exist twenty years ago, and you'll switch between them more regularly.

Bearing all of that in mind, have a go at this light-hearted thought experiment. Don't limit your thinking!

If you had to design a crazy, impossible, perfect job that satisfied your top three motivations, what would it be?

. . . .

. . . .

. . . .

2. Vision Activity: Problem Not Job, aka The Personal Compass

Entrepreneur Derek Sivers argues that to have a single, specific goal in mind can be limiting – because if obstacles keep cropping up to stop us, we eventually abandon this single, specific goal. Instead of a specific goal, he argues that we should spend our lives *pursuing the answer to a problem*. That's our purpose in life. This is a better way to goal set because even when obstacles block our way, we find another route towards solving our chosen problem – of pursuing our purpose.

For example, here are two pretty similar pupils:

Pupil 1 has a super-specific goal: I want to study medicine at Manchester University and become a doctor.

Pupil 2 has a problem that fascinates them: how can we improve healthcare in the UK?

Of course, each pupil will encounter obstacles along their way. But if pupil 1 doesn't get the grades to study medicine at Manchester, the route to their goal is blocked. If the same thing happens to pupil 2, they will find a different route to solving the problem that fascinates them; they may do voluntary work, start a nursing course, choose a degree that covers public healthcare systems or research the politics of healthcare.

Sivers says that if we can express our goals *as problems we're trying to solve*, we always know when we're heading in the right direction and we tend not to be put off by obstacles.

Let's build a compass. Your true north is the problem that most fascinates you – the one you should always be heading towards. Let's call this your *lead problem*. Around true north (north-east, north-west) are other problems that are close to your lead problem – perhaps different versions of your lead problem. If you're heading in this direction you're still doing OK. Around the other compass points (east, south and west) are distractions – things you shouldn't be pursuing, *even if other people think you should*. If you're going in these directions, you'll need to turn back.

Cover the compass points with notes. Problems that interest or fascinate you go at or near your true north. Distractions go elsewhere, with the biggest at the south – the opposite direction to your true north.

Example problems to consider, discuss or discard include:

» How do we make the distribution of wealth in the UK fairer?

» How can we save larger numbers of species from extinction?

» How might we design buildings that increase people's happiness and well-being?

» What are the elements necessary for a superb movie?

» How can we improve pupils' experience of school, college or university?

» How can the design of ______ be improved?

» How can we accelerate our progress towards curing ______?

» How can art be used to improve people's lives?

» What qualities are necessary for huge success in ______?

» How can I create popular, immersive, interactive computer games?

» How can we reduce crime by working with young offenders?

» What qualities make some ______ better than others?

» How can we help people cope with difficult, stressful or traumatic times in their lives?

- What does outstanding parenting/teaching look like?
- How can we discover more about the workings of the universe?
- How do we solve global warming?
- What does augmented/virtual reality mean for media/entertainment/gaming?
- How can we work more efficiently using artificial intelligence?

Once you think you have some interesting problems you'd like to explore further, use the space below to sketch out some next steps. Is there a documentary you could watch, a book you can read, someone you could talk to or ask for advice, or a piece of research you can do to get more information?

Possible problems:

....

....

....

....

....

Possible next steps:

....

....

....

....

....

....

Final Thoughts

Purpose goals tend to be more magnetic and motivating than status goals. Have a look at these examples to see the difference:

- **Purpose:** I see a lot of inequality in the way we are educated and prepared for work, and I want to help tackle that issue.
- **Status:** I want to earn a lot, take long holidays and have a big house.

You might want both of these things. And when times get tough (as they do for everyone at some point!) you'd be forgiven for thinking it would be the status goal that gets you through. But our experience shows it will most likely be the sense of purpose that keeps you moving forwards.

So make sure you're working on developing your sense of purpose. It's going to come in useful!

3. Effort Activity: Mission and Medal

Effort is just a habit. Pupils who have the effort habit have created a weekly routine of repeated activities that allow them to respond to teacher requests (homework) and reinforce learning (independent work). Pupils without the effort habit have little or no routine and respond to work as and when it hits them.

Increasing your levels of effort can be a tiring task because it means moving away from a comfortable and familiar way of working into a less comfortable one. So rewarding yourself for increased levels of effort is hugely important. Parents and teachers might not spot the change in your work patterns right away, so it will be up to you to give yourself a pat on the back.

That's where mission and medal comes in: *the mission is the work, the medal is the reward!* This activity helps you to design and structure an effortful week of work that you can then repeat until it becomes a routine. Pretty soon you won't be the only person rewarding yourself – teachers, tutors and parents will spot your new routine and you'll be in line for some praise!

Step 1: Audit of a Typical Week

Before you design your mission and medal week, you need to figure out what's currently happening. In the space below, record what you do with your time during a typical week. It might be the week just gone or the week you're in. Make a note of what work you do, where you do it and how much productive work gets done in each section of the day.

	Before school (early morning – 7am–8.30am)	**During school (morning and early afternoon – 9am–3pm)**	**After school (twilight – 4pm–5.30pm)**	**Evening (7pm–9.30pm)**
Monday				
Tuesday				
Wednesday				
Thursday				
Friday				
Saturday				
Sunday				

Are there particular slots that work best for you? Are there slots that are hopeless – times when you find it very difficult to work or where you sit down to work but you don't get anything done?

Step 2: Creating a Mission and Medal Week

For five of the seven days, set yourself a *sixty minute mission*. It might be to complete homework, plan ahead, consolidate learning, organise notes, research sixth form colleges, fill out an application or begin a revision guide. Complete the mission all at once or in parts. Choose times of day when you work well – without distractions.

For the same five days, set aside *a medal to be awarded on completion of the mission*. It might be a session on your games console, a TV programme, a football match, some time on social media, something nice to eat or drink or some favourite music. Vary your medals.

Don't forget to assign yourself two *bonus* medals – a mid-weeker to pep you up and a Sunday-nighter to get you feeling good for the week. These medals should be a little larger than your regular medals.

	Before school (early morning – 7am–8.30am)	During school (morning and early afternoon – 9am–3pm)	After school (twilight – 4pm–5.30pm)	Evening (7pm–9.30pm)
Monday				
Mission:				
Medal:				
Tuesday				
Mission:				
Medal:				
Wednesday				
Mission:				
BONUS medal:				
Thursday				
Mission:				
Medal:				
Friday				
Saturday				
Sunday				
Mission:				
BONUS medal:				

In this example, you've been given Friday evening and all day Saturday off. You might want to adjust these depending on what you do with your time – feel free to! Choose exciting medals which make you feel good about the work you've done!

Building a Scoreboard

There's a lot of conflicting research about how long it takes to create a habit. Unless you keep track you'll have no idea. Now you've devised a mission and medal week, you can use a scoreboard as a simple way of helping you with motivation.

We developed this idea after hearing the American comedian Jerry Seinfeld talk about how he writes jokes. He sets himself the goal of writing a joke every day and keeps a diary to check off when he's been successful. His argument is that once you see the days being ticked off, you don't want to see the pattern being broken, so you keep going. After a few weeks, this new behaviour just becomes a habit and you might not even need to think about it – you just do it!

So, for every day you follow your mission and medal programme, you simply tick off the days. You'll need a monthly calendar like the one below.

Sunday	Monday	Tuesday	Wednesday	Thursday	Friday	Saturday
		1	2	3	4	5
6	7	8	9	10	11	12
13	14	15	16	17	18	19
20	21	22	23	24	25	26
27	28	29	30	31		

Final Thoughts

Reactive missions are those set for you by others. It might be your teacher insisting on a finished piece of work by Friday, a tutor asking you to complete an application form, or your mum reminding you to do a job at home.

But what about **proactive missions** – targets you actually set yourself? Try this. Finish the following sentence:

'If I were the perfect student, the kinds of things I might be doing at this time of year include ...'

. . . .

. . . .

. . . .

You don't have to be perfect, of course – no one is. But there might be one or two things in the list above that you *genuinely could do*. Missions you set yourself that will make life so much easier later on in the year.

Why not choose one?

4. Attitude Activity: Growth Mindset

Carol Dweck is one of the world's leading researchers in the field of motivation and is a professor of psychology at Stanford University. She's developed a theory about our attitude towards learning. She says that people generally fall into two categories: a fixed mindset or a growth mindset. Some of the characteristics are shown in the table below.

Fixed mindset	Growth mindset
Feels threatened by the success of others.	Finds lessons and inspiration in the success of others.
Ignores useful feedback.	Learns from criticism.
Sees effort as fruitless or worthless.	Sees effort as the path to mastery.
Gives up easily.	Persists in the face of setbacks.
Avoids challenge.	Embraces challenge.
Desires to look smart.	Desires to learn.

Dweck has developed a questionnaire that helps you to think about your mindset. This can be done here on her mindset website: http://mindsetonline.com/testyourmindset/step1.php.

To give you a quick indication of your mindset try the questionnaire below:

	Item	Mostly agree	Mostly disagree
1	Your intelligence is something very basic that you can't change very much.		
2	You can learn new things but you can't really change how intelligent you are.		
3	No matter how much intelligence you have, you can always change it quite a bit.		
4	You can always substantially change how intelligent you are.		

Scoring and Interpretation

Items 1 and 2 are fixed mindset questions and items 3 and 4 are growth mindset questions. Which mindset did you agree with more? You will be a mixture, but most people lean one way or the other about certain things and at certain times.

What did you learn about yourself?

....

....

....

Where do you have fixed mindset thinking and where do you have more of a growth mindset?

....

....

....

What could you do to change?

. . . .

. . . .

A Quick Test

We often find that pupils express their attitudes towards learning through the things they say. We've listed fifteen phrases we've heard pupils tell us before now. Sort them into fixed and growth mindset statements by ticking the appropriate box.

	Fixed mindset	Growth mindset
I've never been good at maths.		
I just need to get some more practice in.		
I'm hopeless at this.		
Maybe if I was cleverer this would be achievable.		
This doesn't come naturally to me.		
A couple of hours of intense study and I reckon I can crack this problem.		
I've just not got a brain for English/maths/science.		
I'm going to take a break and come back refreshed. I'll make some progress then.		
I'm not a creative person.		
Let me have another go at this – I'll get better.		
I must have missed something. I just need to go back and check I've got this clear in my head.		
I've not totally understood this yet. I'm going to go over it again.		
I can't do this. I'll never be able to do this.		
This topic is impossible. I'm just going to hope it doesn't come up in the exam.		
______ is lucky. They're just naturally brilliant at it. I'm not.		

Finally, if you'd like to learn more about growth mindsets, there are some fun videos here: https://ideas.classdojo.com/b/growth-mindset.

Final Thoughts

You're not permanently a fixed or a growth mindset. In fact, most of us are both at once. Some days, when things go well, we might feel we're improving and growing because of the effort we're putting in. On bad days, we might feel in a fixed mindset state. This is entirely normal. Next time you hit a problem and feel those fixed mindset thoughts coming on, have a look at the phrases above and see if you can borrow one to change your thinking.

October Activities

For many of us, the shiny new feel of the term begins to wear off in October. We often feel things could have gone better, that we've made a few mistakes, and that we're finding things harder than we expected. This is totally normal! What you need in October is a chance to remind yourself of what the goal is, and a moment to reflect on what obstacles seem to be appearing to stop you achieving it. The first of these obstacles will have arrived by now. Some pupils around you might respond by giving up. This month's activities help you carry on, even if you don't feel like it!

5. Vision Activity: The Roadmap

Sometimes setting a goal can feel like a long process. The goals can seem so distant that we don't take any immediate action. Designing a success map can really help with this. A success map is a visual reminder of the journey you're going on. It guides you to where you want to be and warns you about things that might pull you off course.

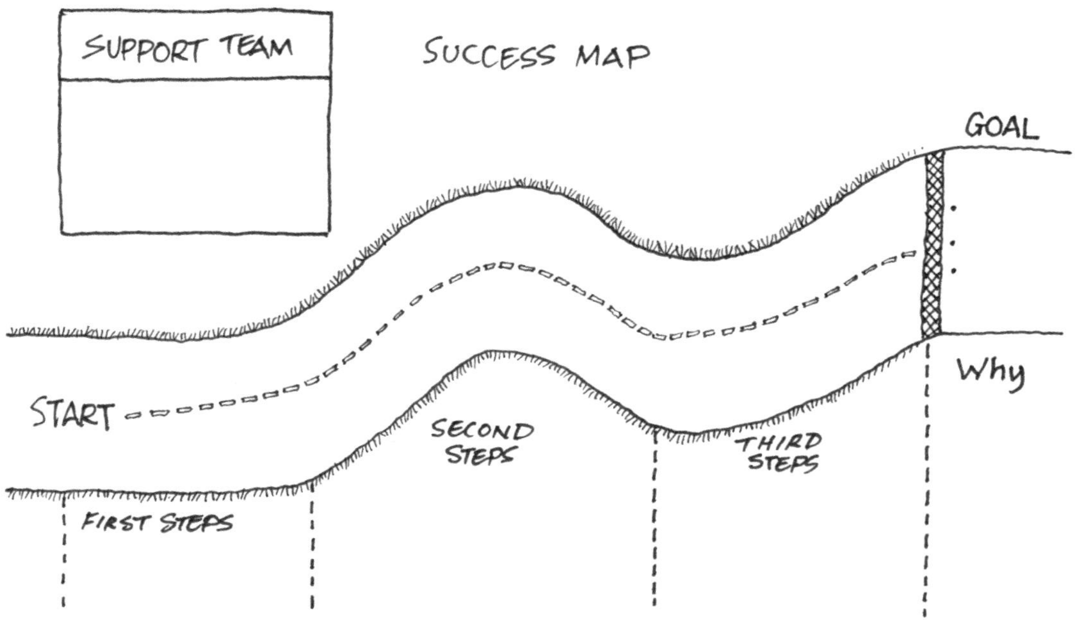

Here's what you need to do. First, you need to go to the end of the map and write down the goal you want to achieve. In the same box it's useful to include the date by which you want to achieve your goal. Underneath the goal box you'll see 'why'. Here you write why achieving the goal is important to you.

Next, you need to break down the goal into a series of steps in a journey. You might think about these steps as a series of days, weeks or even months. Represent them as a road or pathway – some sort of track that takes you through the difficulties towards a conclusion.

Look at how this university student has used a dotted line to indicate the journey of her boat between the islands in this map:

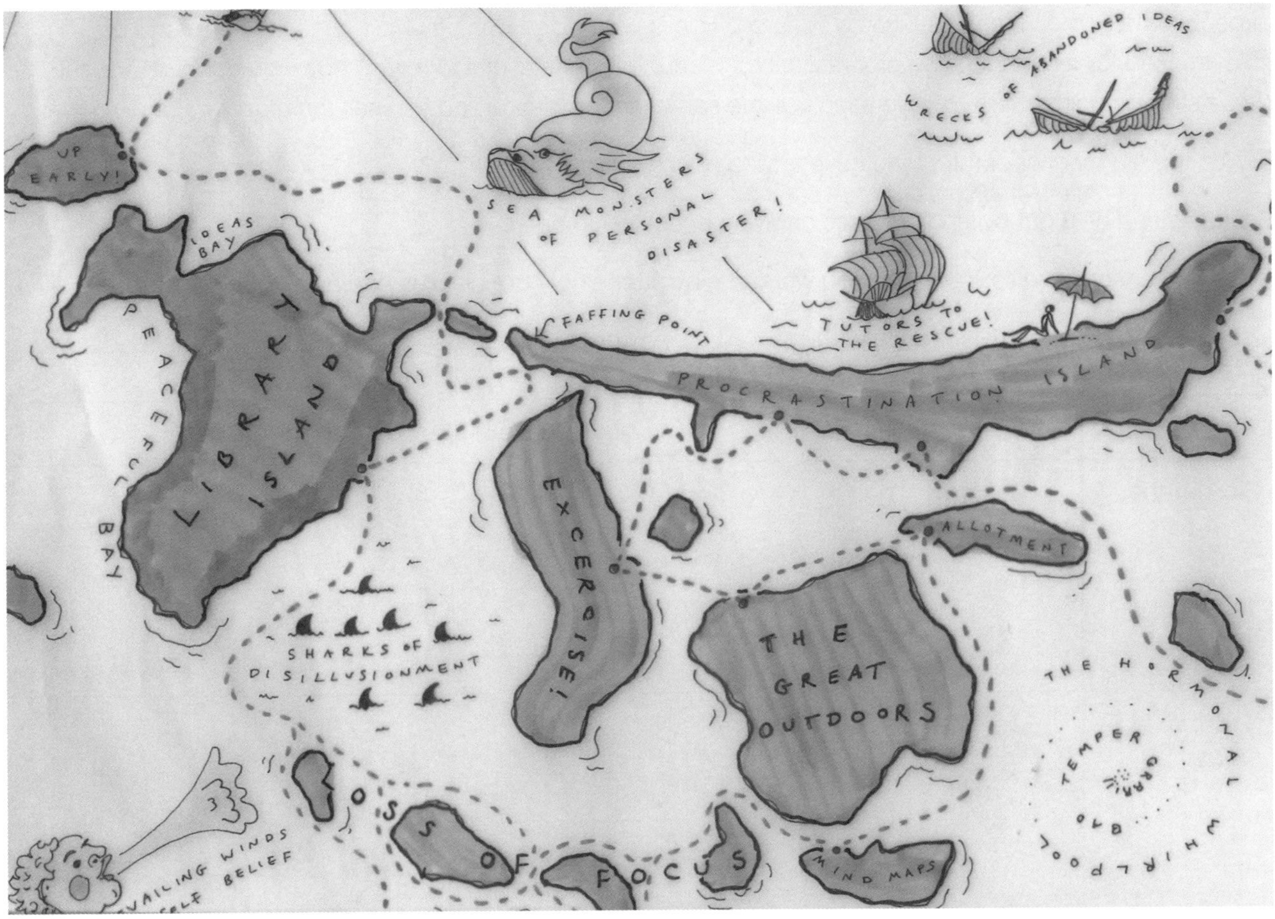

Credit: Jo Phillips (used with permission).

There are two main elements here – the positive and the negative. Have a look at how the student emphasises positive things that are going to help: 'Peaceful Bay', 'Exercise', 'Up Early!', 'Mind Maps' and 'Tutors to the Rescue!' And hazards to watch out for: 'Loss of Focus', 'Sharks of Disillusionment' and 'Sea Monsters of Personal Disaster!'.

You can do the same on your map:

- **Mapping your support.** Surround your pathway with good things that will encourage and help you. Rewards, celebrations and holidays all need marking on the map. Think about the people who might support you too. Could you ask friends, a mentor or your parents/guardian? Write the names of these people in your 'support team' box.
- **Mapping your challenges.** Here you should include the things you're going to need to watch out for. They should be specific to you – your bad habits! It might be laziness, procrastination, worry or distraction.

Unlike the example above, we've found it useful to add dates to the map so you know what happens when in the year ahead.

Once done, it's a good idea to keep your map on display somewhere that you can always see it. This will help to remind you of the steps that need to be completed to reach that destination in the distance!

Final Thoughts

It doesn't matter whether you travel by land, air or sea, when you are working towards your goals you can expect some bumps that knock you off course. This is normal, so don't feel too stressed if you end up shipwrecked for a short time on procrastination island. It can be useful to record how you got over or past these sticking points. This way, you can use the same strategy if you find yourself there again. For example:

» Was there a teacher or tutor who gave advice or changed your thinking?

» Did a friend help out by lending notes or giving encouragement?

» Did you change the time or place you worked – by attending extra classes or staying behind after school?

Use the table below to reflect on how things have gone and how you dealt with the bumps in the road so far.

	Bumps	How I got past them
First steps		
Second steps		
Third steps		

6. Systems Activity: The Weekly Planner

Most pupils have used a calendar for planning their revision at some point. But even at the start of a year, it's worth taking stock of your week. What does a typical week look like for you? Where are the gaps (if there are any) or are you over-committed?

We recently did this with a pupil who was starting to feel very stressed. When he filled in the weekly planner it became very clear why – he literally didn't have a spare minute! To find additional time to get on top of his schoolwork, the only option would have been for him to sleep less (not something we would recommend!). It was apparent that he was committed to too many activities: he was attending swimming sessions three times a week, including all day on Saturday, he helped out at a kids activity session on a Tuesday evening and he was working for his uncle in his shop for eight hours during the week. He was clearly going to burn out before he got to Christmas!

Current vs. Preferred

The first step of this exercise is to record your weekly activities. You can get creative here and use different colours for different activities. Make a note of everything you're doing with your time – school, of course, but also commitments to classes, sport, jobs, helping out at home and so on.

Preferred Weekly Activities

	Before school (early morning – 7am–8.30am)	**During school (morning and early afternoon – 9am–3pm)**	**After school (twilight – 4pm–5.30pm)**	**Evening (7pm–9.30pm)**
Monday				
Tuesday				
Wednesday				
Thursday				
Friday				
Saturday				
Sunday				

The next step is to decide: are you happy with your week? Are there things you'd like to change?

If there are things you would like to change, you need to plan out your preferred week, then complete the table below. This will help you to think through the advantages and disadvantages of making the changes. If the positives outweigh the negatives, you know what needs to be done!

Advantages of making changes	**Disadvantages of making changes**
....	....
....	....
....	....
....	....

Disadvantages of not making changes	Advantages of not making changes
....	....
....	....
....	....
....	....

Final Thoughts

This is an ideal opportunity to reflect on the time you have and the way you're using it. Have a look at the questions that follow and see if they help you make some decisions about how to change your week:

How much of your time is spent doing things you *have* to do?

....

....

How much of your time is spent doing things you *want* to do?

....

....

If you had more time, what would you add?

....

If you could remove one thing (except 'school'!), what would it be and why?

....

....

If you had to pick one thing you were 'doing too much of', what would it be?

....

....

Have you got enough time for rest/sleep/friends etc.?

....

....

Is there an area you'd like to allocate more time to?

....

....

7. Vision Activity: The Rule of Three

We borrowed this activity from Jack Canfield's book *The Success Principles* (2005). He is also the author of the 'Chicken Soup for the Soul' series (we would recommend *Chicken Soup for the Teenage Soul* – it's full of supportive stories, reassuring advice and cracking ideas).

Canfield employs the useful analogy of chopping down a tree when trying to achieve your goals. He says that if you take a very sharp axe and take five swings at a tree every day, no matter how big the tree, eventually it will come down. It's the same with any goal you set. If you take a few small steps every month towards achieving your goal, eventually you'll get there, no matter how big the goal.

Canfield almost makes it sound inevitable. It makes you think: the reason people don't achieve their dreams isn't that they lack a dream, it's that they just don't take any action. *A dream is just a dream unless you take action!*

This activity might seem simple, but we guarantee it's one of the most effective tools we have ever used.

All you have to do is take three steps every half-term towards achieving your long-term goal. It's that simple. You have to decide the steps you are going to take and then commit to doing them.

First, remind yourself of your long-term goal:

My goal is: ____.

Then list all the actions that are going to take you closer to achieving that goal. Remember, it's only three small steps per half-term – that's roughly one every two weeks.

	Action steps	Completed
Sept–Oct	....	
Nov–Dec	....	
Jan–Feb	....	
Mar–April	....	

April–May	. . . .	
June–July	. . . .	

When you've completed the table, it's important that you keep it somewhere you can see it. Stick it up in your room or study area. You might find it useful to share it with a friend or parent and ask them to check up on your progress.

Final Thoughts

What if I don't know exactly what the steps are?

Here's where research comes in. We've worked with hundreds of students who've wanted to do something we didn't know much about. Over the years we've had to find out how to become an actor, how to get into graphic design, how to get a work-shadowing position at a games design company, and so on.

Remember this – whatever you're trying to achieve, the chances are someone else has done it before you. It might be someone in the year above you, an older brother or sister, or a tutor or teacher. If there isn't someone close to home, who could you contact more remotely, through email or social media?

Someone nearby who might be able to help:

. . . .

Someone I might contact remotely:

. . . .

8. Systems Activity: Chunking Steps

The higher you progress up the school, the more likely it is that you are going to get pieces of work that require more than one sitting to complete. This means that you will be unlikely to sit down and finish the whole activity or project in one go. Gone are the Key Stage 3 days when most homework could be completed within fifteen or twenty minutes!

Sooner or later you're going to get a piece of homework or coursework that you know is going to take a few hours to complete. At first this can be quite daunting. Often, when we are faced with a large piece of work like this we procrastinate (put it off) because we're not sure where to start.

There's an old Chinese proverb that says, 'A journey of a thousand miles begins with a single step.' Chunking will help you to take that first step.

Here's how it works. Let's imagine that you've decided to run a marathon in a year's time. There are a number of things you might need to do (run a lot of miles is the obvious one!), but you can't go straight out and run twenty-six miles. You first need to break down all the tasks you might need to do:

» Buy some trainers
» Find a coach
» Enter a race
» Join a running club
» Run a 10K

This would be the start of the list – there's much more than we've listed here. The second step is to set yourself some milestones (what you need to have done and by when).

You can use the same process with a long and challenging piece of work. Here are the steps you might need to take:

» **Step 1:** Identify the goal. How will you know when the task is complete? What will it look like? When will it be?

....

....

....

» **Step 2:** Write down everything you will need to do to complete the task – everything you can think of from the start to the end. Your ideas might come out in a crazy order – that's fine! You can sort them out later.

....

....

....

....

....

....

....

....

....

....

» **Step 3:** Decide the order of activities using the diagram below, adding them to the steps. Don't forget to include a deadline for each step.

1. ....
2. ....
3. ....
4. ....
5. ....
6. ....
7. ....
8. ....
9. ....
10. ....

Now pin this up somewhere clear and prominent, and check it regularly!

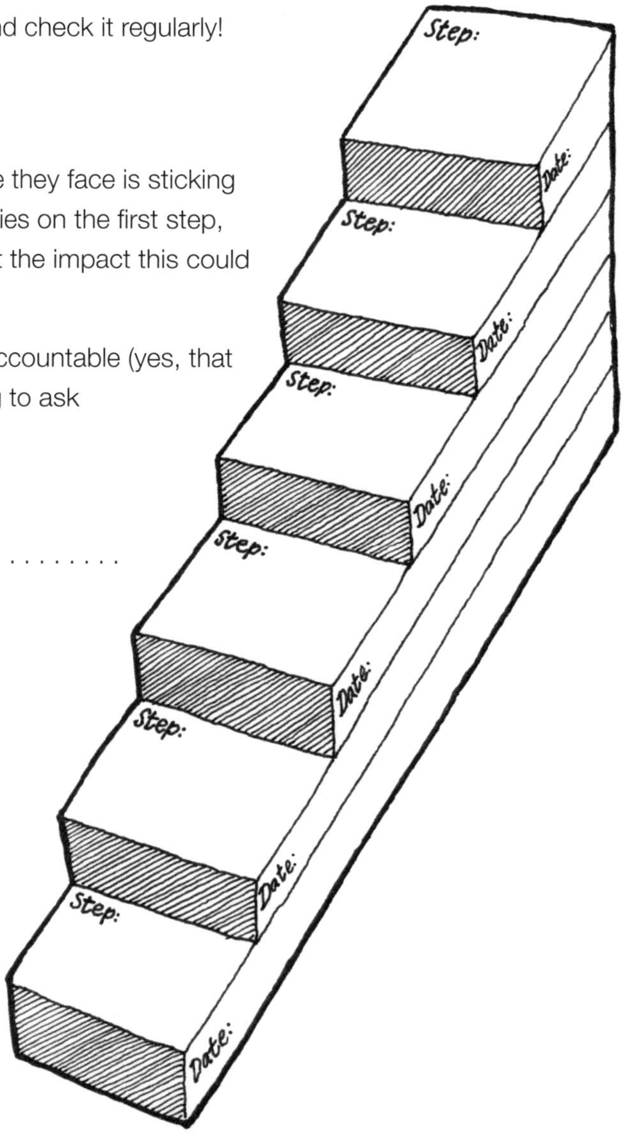

Final Thoughts

When pupils use the chunking activity, one challenge they face is sticking to the steps at each stage. If you don't do the activities on the first step, it's unlikely that you'll meet the deadline. Think about the impact this could have on your time and your stress levels!

One useful strategy is to get someone to hold you accountable (yes, that means checking on you!). Decide who you are going to ask and then share your plan with them.

Who might be good at holding you accountable?

....

9. Vision Activity: Grit

We often hear about the term 'grit', but what does it mean and can you measure it?

Grit is about having passion and perseverance for a long-term goal. It's an idea that has been developed by Angela Duckworth, a professor at the University of Pennsylvania. She's spent years looking at grit and how it can be developed. Most people have at least one area where they might have shown grit. For example, you might have started dance classes when you were young and still be dancing ten years later, you might have persisted in developing as a footballer, have been drawing and painting in your spare time for years or have learned how to play a musical instrument.

One of the best-known examples of grit is the author J. K. Rowling. Joanne Rowling first got the idea for the Harry Potter series on a delayed train from Manchester to King's Cross station in London. At the time, Rowling was a single parent and living on state benefits. She often did her writing in cafes in Edinburgh, with her young daughter next to her in a pram, because her apartment was so cold and she couldn't afford the heating. She worked on the first Harry Potter book for five years! It was rejected by at least a dozen publishers before being accepted by Bloomsbury. The Harry Potter series has now sold over 450 million copies worldwide. J. K. Rowling's Harvard commencement speech describes the perseverance to continue her love of writing while experiencing professional rejection and doubt. You can watch it here: https://www.youtube.com/watch?v=wHGqp8lz36c.

It's worth remembering that there's no such thing as an overnight success. Most successful people have usually spent years working behind the scenes to develop their craft. They've often shown passion and perseverance for many years before anyone recognised their work. This is true grit.

So, How Gritty Are You?

Below is a version of the Grit Scale developed by Angela Duckworth (Duckworth, 2016, p. 55). Don't think about the questions too much. Just go for your gut feeling and answer the questions in relation to most people.

	Not at all like me = 1	**Not much like me = 2**	**Somewhat like me = 3**	**Mostly like me = 4**	**Very much like me = 5**
1. New ideas and projects distract me from previous ones.					
2. Setbacks don't discourage me. I don't give up easily.					
3. I often set a goal but later pursue a different one.					
4. I am a hard worker.					
5. I have difficulty maintaining my focus on projects that take more than a few months to complete.					
6. I finish whatever I begin.					

	Not at all like me = 1	Not much like me = 2	Somewhat like me = 3	Mostly like me = 4	Very much like me = 5
7. My interests change from year to year.					
8. I am diligent. I never give up.					
9. I have been obsessed with an idea or project for a short time but later lost interest.					
10. I have overcome setbacks to conquer an important challenge.					

To calculate your grit score, add up all the points for the boxes and divide by 10. The highest score you can get is 5 (very gritty) and the lowest score is 1 (not at all gritty).

You could discuss your findings with your parents, tutor or friends. Do you think the score is accurate?

Final Thoughts

When you've discussed the questionnaire answer the questions below:

1. When have I been most gritty?

....

....

....

2. How could I become grittier with my schoolwork?

....

....

....

Remember, you are only young so your grit score hasn't fully developed yet. You might also find it useful to watch Duckworth's famous TED Talk on grit at: https://www.ted.com/talks/angela_lee_duckworth_grit_the_power_of_passion_and_perseverance.

November Activities

With mock exams coming up, November is one of the months that really count. It's not easy, though – the nights get darker, the weather's terrible and that December holiday still seems a long way off. So feeling pretty gloomy isn't unusual. This month's activities tend to focus on how to organise getting things done, which is something that will make you feel better! You'll be doing homework and classwork of course, but this is a month for taking on some extra commitments – you might re-organise your notes in preparation for an exam, struggle with a difficult topic, or call in a favour to get ahead in a subject. The resources here help you plan how you'll get that revision started.

10. Practice Activity: Building Independent Learning

For some pupils the only work they ever do has been set by their teacher: do you ever do more?

We've found that the top performing pupils are usually setting their own work if their teacher hasn't set it for them. This can be hard, though, particularly if you aren't sure exactly what work to set yourself. Teachers quite often say to pupils that they should be doing 'independent learning' or 'reading around the subject'. But what does that actually mean?

We would suggest that you get much more specific and design your independent learning so that you know exactly what you should be doing and how long it should take you. (Some teachers provide their pupils with this sort of activity, so it might be an activity you can skip. If not, read on.)

Five Independent Learning Activities

For each of your GCSE subjects we suggest that you design five activities.

First, identify the topic. What is it you'd like to spend some more time on?

Second, what are you going to do? Watch a YouTube video, read a book or do some online research? Use this table of suggestions to get you started, and choose five.

Comparing your work with that of pupils who get higher grades.
Making a clear, visual overview of a course, connecting all the content in a huge diagram/mind-map.
Creating flashcards as a memory aid.
Reading lots of exam questions and seeing if you can recognise 'types' or 'genres' of question.
Asking for extra work to be assessed and carefully reading the feedback you get.
Creating a glossary of key words with definitions.

Expanding class notes with reference to textbooks.
Representing complicated information visually using a table, chart or diagram.
Reading through an examiners' report and making a list of dos and don'ts.
Choosing a specific area of difficulty and discussing it in detail with a friend.
Planning responses to past exam questions.
Borrowing someone else's class notes and using them to expand yours.
Finding a brilliant course textbook and reading a chapter, making notes as you go.
Watching online videos and interacting with associated VLE resources.
Arranging a meeting with an older student or sibling who has done the course before.
Writing for twenty minutes under timed conditions.

Third, where do you need to go to get access to the resources?

Finally, what activity are you going to do? Remember, doing some active work is going to be more beneficial than passive activities.

Now you've got a plan, complete the table below for each subject. The example below is for GCSE sociology.

Subject: Sociology

Topic	What	Where	Activity
1. Research methods	Watch the first YouTube video on statistics	https://www.youtube.com/watch?v=PDjS20kic54	Make a mind-map while watching

Now use some of these others to plan what your independent study might look like for some of your other courses.

Subject:

Topic	What	Where	Activity
....	....	....	....
....	....	....	....
....	....	....	....
....	....	....	....
....	....	....	....
....	....	....	....
....	....	....	....

Subject:

Topic	What	Where	Activity

Subject:

Topic	What	Where	Activity

November Activities

Subject:

Topic	What	Where	Activity

Subject:

Topic	What	Where	Activity

Final Thoughts

This activity works well with the weekly planner. Could you timetable a specific time each week to work on your independent learning?

11. Systems Activity: Three Types of Attention

Everyone's day moves through phases, and you're probably no different – there are times when you're fired up and raring to go, there are times when your energy levels are just average and there are times when you feel your attention is low and your motivation dips.

These three phases happen to everyone during a working day. You're not unusual if you have low energy levels or can't concentrate; if you catch yourself looking around you and seeing others hard at work, remember they're no different to you – they're just in a different phase of their day.

Some people can predict when they're going to be feeling fired up (it might be the mornings, it might be after breakfast or after exercise) and when they're going to feel slower. Others haven't noticed a pattern, but once they pay attention they see one emerging. For others, it's totally random.

Graham Allcott, founder of Think Productive (http://thinkproductive.co.uk), uses the following definitions for the three states:

1. Proactive attention (fully focused, fired up, feeling fresh).
2. Active attention (plugged in, ticking along nicely).
3. Inactive attention (flagging, fried, foggy).

He argues that really successful people get work done in all three states. They don't give up when they're in state 3, they just switch tasks.

Make a list of all the tasks you've got on your plate at the moment. Think of everything – homework, reading, essays, revision, upcoming tests, college interviews, etc.

Now categorise them. Complex and challenging tasks go in 'proactive attention'. When you feel fully focused, fired up and fresh, you tackle those. Regular tasks go in 'active attention'. They're tasks to get on with when you feel you're ticking along nicely. Repetitive tasks that are pretty easy go in 'inactive attention'. When you're feeling fried or foggy, you switch to those tasks.

Proactive attention	**Active attention**	**Inactive attention**
....	....	....
....	....	....
....	....	....
....	....	....
....	....	....

Keep the list with you for a week or two. Whenever you're about to start working:

» Check your energy levels. Sit still for a second and listen to your body. Decide which attention state you're in.

» Review the list of tasks you've got to do that suit your attention level. If there are none in that column, find one from the next column and tackle it.

After a week or two, see whether you can observe patterns in your attention levels. Really good learners have noticed these patterns in themselves and sequence their tasks beforehand.

Final Thoughts

One way to log your attention is by colour coding. Use green for proactive attention, amber for active attention, and red for inactive. You could use a grid that looked something like this:

	Monday	Tuesday	Wednesday	Thursday	Friday	Saturday	Sunday
8–10am							
10am–12pm							
1–3pm							
3–5pm							
6–8pm							
8–10pm							

We've found that certain people move through predictable phases of attention. Some start the day full of energy, but dip slowly as the day goes on. Others respond to food (!), feeling more sluggish after lunch, for example. Others have worked out ways to jump into proactive attention before doing an important piece of work.

This last skill is really valuable. *If you can boost your attention, you can get more work done in less time*. Try experimenting with boosting attention. We've spoken to students who do the following:

Exercise just before work: A run, a walk, a quick jog around the block, even an intense burst of star jumps!

Listen to music just before work: A loud burst of motivating music with headphones on.

Other pre-work rituals: Some students talk about tidying their work spaces to get 'in the zone', or having a hot shower, or getting changed or a quick ten-minute burst of game-playing (bright, colourful puzzlers work way better than long, complex strategy or role-playing games).

Use the space below to record your experiments and plans:

. . . .

. . . .

. . . .

. . . .

. . . .

12. Attitude Activity: Network Audits

Sometimes it's easy to forget how many people want to help you succeed. Each of us has a significant network of support around us, but it's a natural tendency sometimes to think, 'If I ask for help it must mean I'm failing. I need to do this alone.'

But seeking help just makes everything easier. So don't believe the story that goes, 'One day I'll have to stand on my own two feet. I may as well start now.' As you grow up and face new challenges, there will *always* be people around you who can help; someone who's done it before and can give you some advice. Nowadays, that help is just a search engine away – you can contact experts in thousands of fields through social media. You could spend a very successful life continually asking for help!

But still the myth persists that we must do it alone. This activity should support you in auditing (that means listing and organising) every single person who could be on your team. And from there, you can decide who you need to help you with some upcoming challenges.

You're the dot at the top of the pyramid and underneath you is a team of people all waiting for the chance to support you. First, make a list of everyone you can think of that fits into the categories.

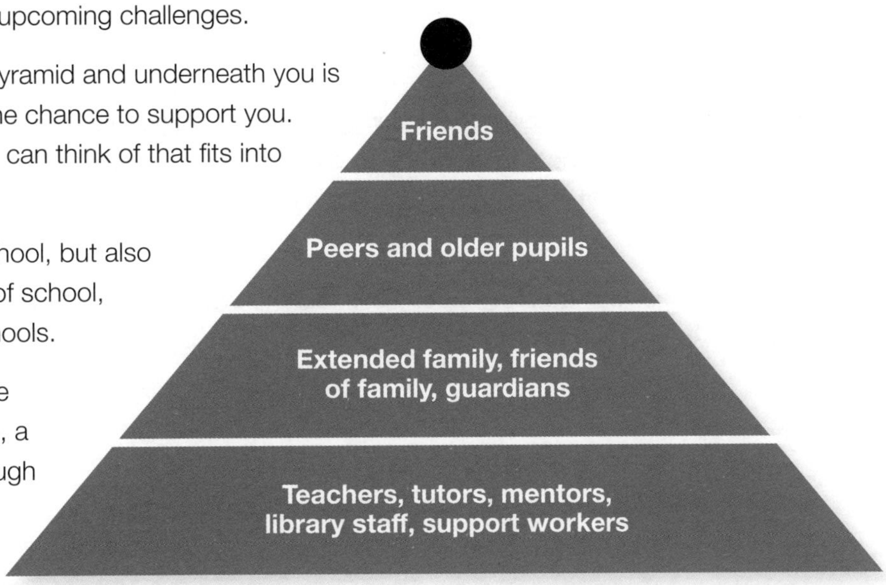

- Think of friends you have at school, but also those you might have outside of school, on social media or at other schools.
- Who among your peers has the potential to help you out? Who, a few years older, has gone through this already? Who's an expert on the subjects you're struggling with? Which of your friends has an older brother or sister you could speak to?
- Think about your parents, of course, but also aunties, uncles, cousins and family friends.
- You attend a school where every paid member of staff has a genuine interest in helping you improve. Your first thoughts might be your own teachers, but what about other staff members – librarians, tutors and mentors? All of them will have something to offer.

Friends:

Peers:

Family:

. . . .

. . . .

. . . .

Teachers, tutors and other professionals:

. . . .

. . . .

. . . .

Now you've made your list, highlight or underline those people you've relied heavily on before. You've hassled them a lot – gone back to them to seek help and advice. Or are there none of these individuals whatsoever? Are you trying to do everything on your own? Are there any layers where you've consulted no one at all? Are there any untapped resources in your network?

Next, list three things you need to get done this month, and for each of the tasks, attach the name of one person who could help you to get it done quicker:

Task one:

. . . .

Task two:

. . . .

Task three:

. . . .

Finally, go and see them!

Note: This works the other way too. What if someone comes asking you for help? Pay it forward. Give the time. Build up an account of goodwill you can draw on when you need it.

Final Thoughts

Some very successful people become successful *precisely because* they asked for help from so many people. The entrepreneur and writer Tim Ferriss' most recent book is 2017's *Tribe of Mentors*. Ferriss finds himself at 40 years old, a successful author and investor, wanting help and support with so many queries and questions that he decides to ask for advice from a hundred people. He emails them all and asks them what they might do in his shoes.

The result is a book full of amazing and inspiring advice and guidance.

So don't lose the opportunity to ask for help!

13. Effort Activity: Looking Under the Rocks, aka Four Steps Forward

Sometimes facing the reality of a situation can seem daunting. We all hide from the facts sometimes – we know something needs changing but it can seem easier just not to make the change. Here's a good metaphor for exploring this further. Have you ever wandered down a beach and lifted up some rocks? It can be quite scary but good fun.

You never quite know what you are going to find. To begin with there seems to be no sign of life. Then you lift a rock and all sorts of squidgy creatures come out – little worms, crabs, snails, sea anemones or even the odd fish. More often than not people put the rock back down and move on, preferring not to spend too much time looking at what's underneath. But sometimes in life we have to look under the rocks to make progress.

This technique is used a lot in business. A researcher and writer called Jim Collins, in his book *Good to Great*, found that all successful companies face the brutal facts of reality, looking under the rocks for problems, even when they don't want to!

This activity is going to feel uncomfortable but by the end of it you will have a plan to make things better.

The first step is to identify any issues you think are under the rocks. This means taking some time and being really, brutally honest with yourself.

Things I need to change to improve my study at school ...
....
....
....
....

The second step requires a group of four friends. Position yourself so that you are facing the group. You are then going to share your issue for change and the rest of the group are going to ask you questions and maybe offer some solutions. Listen carefully during this feedback. We quite often think that we can't change something simply because we have run out of ideas.

Now you've had a long, critical look at your progress you might be feeling pretty bruised. Take a break, go for a walk, watch TV, treat yourself to ice cream.

Once you have, it's time for the third step: time to start considering some action. What exactly can you do to improve matters?

Four Steps Forward

You might know all about origami, the Japanese art of paper folding. Those who do it can make beautiful and complex 3D models, many of which look incredible and even have moving parts. Despite these amazing constructions, the process is just a series of simple steps repeated over and over again. Every origami masterpiece begins with a single fold in a piece of paper, followed by another and another and another.

It's the same with academic learning. Sometimes we might look at a pupil who's way ahead of us and think they've achieved something impossible. But remember: all that pupil has done is execute a repeated series of steps over and over again.

For now, forget the big picture and instead concentrate on the immediate. We've found that deciding on your *next four steps* is the best way to do this.

What could you do next? Consider some of the following:

1. Calling in a favour from a friend or peer.
2. Starting a big project you've been putting off for a while.
3. Handing a piece of homework in early.
4. Rescuing a project that's behind schedule.
5. Asking five questions of a teacher to clarify a problem you've been trying to ignore.
6. Seeking a book/study guide recommendation.
7. Completing a one-hour reread and reorganise of notes on any topic.
8. Sending five emails asking for support, help, advice or an opportunity.
9. Seeing another pupil and asking them to talk you through a topic.
10. Borrowing someone else's notes.
11. Attending a support class or revision session.
12. Handing in a redone piece of work.
13. Reviewing your feedback to look for patterns.
14. Tidying your resources and summarising a topic on one sheet of A4.

OK, you've looked under the rocks and admitted a few things you aren't proud of. You've asked for extra feedback and suggestions from helpful friends. And you've considered our list of fourteen possible actions.

Now, choose the four things you're going to do and write them in the table below. Put a date next to each. And choose a reward for yourself – something you're going to do to celebrate getting your improvements underway. Make it a motivating one!

1	**2**	**3**	**4**	**Jackpot! Reward:**
....	....	....	....	....

Final Thoughts

This can be a tricky activity. It's not easy looking under the rocks, but once you've done it and taken action you'll feel much better about things.

December Activities

This month's activities are exam focused. That's because most pupils in Year 11 take mock exams in December – the results of which often go on application forms for colleges. There are ways of revising that work better than others, but as learners we're often loyal to old habits. *This has always worked for me before*, you might think, *so I'll keep on doing it*. Some of the activities here might seem new and strange, and your first response might be to reject them. But research shows they work. You should give them a try. They might feel harder and more challenging than your usual methods of revision, but they'll take you further too.

14. Practice Activity: The Practice Questionnaire

We've found there is a strong link between the kind of revision someone does and the outcomes they get. So, which pupil will do better in an exam?

» Pupil 1 does fifteen hours of revision – all of it reading through class notes.

» Pupil 2 only does ten hours of revision – two hours making mind-maps, two hours creating flashcards of key terms, three hours writing timed essays, two hours working through past papers and looking for patterns in the questions asked, and half an hour doing the hardest question they could find, followed by half an hour talking it through with their teacher. Then they spend five hours shopping with their friends and watching TV.

You too can make less mean more. Try this questionnaire:

Name: . . . . Subject: . . . .

1. How many hours of independent work do you do on your subjects outside of class? Please state the time spent on each subject.

   . . . .

2. What sort of activities do you do? Use the table below:

		Always	Sometimes	Never
Reading through class notes	C			
Using resources on the school's VLE	C			
Using course textbooks	C			
Mind-maps/diagrams	C			
Making/remaking class notes	C			

		Always	Sometimes	Never
Highlighting/colour coding	C			
Flashcards	C			
Using a revision wall to display your learning	C			
Writing exam answers under timed conditions	S			
Reading model answers	S			
Using past exam questions and planning answers	S			
Marking your own work to a mark scheme	F			
Studying mark schemes or examiners' reports	F			
Working with other pupils in groups/pairs	F			
Comparing model answers against your own work	F			
Creating your own exam questions	F			
Handing in extra exam work for marking	F			
One-to-one discussions with teachers/tutors	F			

3. Additional activities not mentioned above:

4. Write a brief account of what you do if you can't understand something (e.g. try again, read textbooks, check the school's VLE, see teachers, ask other pupils).

You will notice some activities have a 'C' next to them – these are the *content* techniques. Some activities have an 'S' next to them – these are the *skills* techniques. Others have an 'F' next to them – these are the *feedback* techniques.

Notice in our example that pupil 1 only does content revision, while pupil 2 does all three stages and then takes some time off. In our experience, pupil 2 will pretty much always get a better grade than pupil 1. And they put in fewer hours.

Have a look at the activities associated with each stage of revision and draw up a list of three or four you aren't doing at the moment but that you'd like to try:

1. ....

2. ....

3. ....

4. ....

Final Thoughts

We've found that pupils who get the best grades practise in a wider variety of ways. Our top performers often had ten or more ticks in the always column, pretty evenly spread across C, S and F.

Pupils who got lower grades nearly always had fewer ticks in the always column, often something like four or five. They were much more restricted in the way they practised, often spending hours repeating the same limited range of activities.

Aim to increase your ticks in the always column to ten.

15. Effort Activity: The Three 'Hows' of Independent Work

We've worked with thousands of pupils who are great at designing revision; they create amazing revision and independent work plans that fill every minute of the day, but then just don't follow through on the plan.

It's something we've all done; if you have too, don't beat yourself up about it. Why do we procrastinate? Why do we avoid putting the effort in?

This might surprise you, but saying that you are going to do some 'independent work' or 'revision' is actually part of the problem. When you say that you are going to revise (as far as your brain is concerned), it's vague and ambiguous. When your brain thinks that you are about to do something that's vague and ambiguous it will often start to come up with reasons why you shouldn't do it (which can be quite useful). This probably sounds a bit odd, but your brain starts thinking that this isn't really a well thought-out plan. It's not sure what you are going to be doing, or how, and your brain starts to get you thinking that it might not even work. Then you procrastinate.

So how do you get past this?

It's quite a simple strategy but we promise you it works. You have to get specific. Here's how. Before every independent work session or revision session you have to sit down and answer these three questions:

1. How am I going to revise/work?
   Here you have to be specific about the *how* (what strategy you are going to use) and also *what* you are going to revise. This means identifying specifically the topics you are going to cover, and the activities you're going to do to cover the work.
2. How long am I going to revise/work for?
   Be very clear about the time. If you are doing active revision this shouldn't be any longer than two hours. Remember to build in short (ten minute) breaks every forty minutes. Use Twenty-Five Minute Sprints (page 62) to help structure sessions, and it becomes even easier to beat procrastination.
3. How will I know if I've made progress?
   How are you going to test yourself? If you just sit for two hours passively reading your notes you will have no idea if you have made any progress, so you'll need to test yourself in some way. It might be a set of questions you answer, a mini-lecture that you give to yourself, or short-answer questions you're going to do under timed conditions towards the end of the session.

You can get into the habit of doing this mentally, but to start with complete the table below before you begin every independent work or revision session. Then start!

How am I going to revise/work?	....

How long am I going to revise/ work for?	....
How will I know if I've made progress?	....

Final Thoughts

Once you've done this a few times, you might start noticing certain revision sessions that feel easier than others.

Watch out for sessions that feel too straightforward and too easy. Often they're the result of planning an activity that isn't very challenging, and that is quite simple and often pretty boring to complete. When you're working, try asking yourself, 'Would my strictest teachers let me get away with doing this for an hour?'

If the answer is 'No', it might be that you need to step up the challenge a little. That way, you can get more done in less time.

16. Practice Activity: It's Time to Teach, aka CASTT

Cal Newport is a professor of computer science at Georgetown University, Washington, DC. He's written a few great books to help pupils achieve the best grades they can. It's worth taking a look at his website: www.calnewport.com.

In addition to teaching pupils at university, he's been fascinated by the strategies pupils use to help them get great grades. He suggests that when it comes to revision there are two types: active recall and passive recall.

» Active recall is *actively trying to understand and synthesise the information by teaching it*.
(Don't worry – you don't need your own class of Year 7s for this! You can do it alone, or to someone else; a friend, a parent or a sibling.)

» Passive recall, by contrast, is just sitting passively reading your notes.

Newport makes a bold statement: *active recall is the only revision strategy that counts*! He argues that there are three huge benefits to this type of super-charged revision:

1. It's very effective.
2. It saves time.
3. It's difficult and mentally uncomfortable. (Don't worry, it's supposed to be!)

So how do you do it?

We've set a little challenge for you. We want you to *only* use active recall for the next test you have in one of your subjects. During this time you are not allowed to use any other strategy. You are either doing active recall or preparing for it. No sitting comfortably and reading your notes!

If you're interested in trying this experiment, you'll need to start about three weeks before a test or mock exam and you'll need to set aside a few hours each week. Block the time out on your planner before you start, then follow our CASTT process.

Week 1: Collect and Arrange (C and A)

This week is preparation week – we call it 'collect and arrange' because it gives you chance to gather everything you need and make sense of it. The first thing you need to do is identify and collect the topics that you will be tested on; make a list of them. A syllabus might help here, or a list provided by a teacher. Once you've got your list of topics, you're really in business. You know the size of the job ahead of you.

Once you've identified and collected together your topics you need to arrange or organise your notes for the topics, and try to condense the material into a small space – one or two sides of A4, for example. It might be useful to use mind-maps for this, or other graphic organisers like tables, lists, bullet points or flow charts. Consider trying one of our faves – a Nine-Box Grid (page 64).

Weeks 2 and 3: Search (S) and Teach (T)

Now you'll need to do a search for any past paper questions connected to the topics you've collected and arranged in week 1. You're trying to find example tests that are as close to the one you're going to experience in the test coming up – in other words, to reproduce the test experience! Search everywhere. Do you already have exam questions in your books or folders? Did your teachers hand some out? Are there some on your school's online resources or in the school library? Maybe an exam-board website can help. You want to be the person who has searched out more exam questions than anyone else!

Once you've got your hoard, you can begin teaching – in other words, it's active recall only! Grab your exam question, write it in the middle of a piece of A4 and plan an answer around it. Now: imagine you're a teacher, explaining how to answer the question to your class. Imagine this class really need things explaining slowly and clearly, and you're at the front with a whiteboard, explaining exactly what to do, how to do it and why to do it.

In week 2 it might be that you try to teach the information with only yourself present. Have the mind-map in front of you and aim to recall and explain as much information as possible without looking. It might be useful to cover up your mind-map and then just expose sections if you are struggling. Don't worry if it's not perfect – it won't be at first. Remember that you have to speak out loud. It will feel odd at first but just keep going.

In week 3 you might try teaching with an audience. Give someone the mind-map while you try to recall. Get the observer to make a note of anything you miss. Then try it again.

Finally: Test (T)

Finally, to check that the process is working effectively you must test yourself. Put away all the mind-maps and notes from weeks 1, 2 and 3, clear your desk and put your phone on airplane settings. Now, write a response to the exam question under timed conditions.

Take it to a teacher for marking, or check it against a mark scheme.

And that's it! Active recall in four steps. It might not always feel easy or relaxed, but it's quick, intense, and effective. Remember CASTT next time you need to practise for a test or exam!

Final Thoughts

Whenever you trial a different method of revising it's worth testing how effective it is! If you're not convinced, do one day of revising using your usual techniques and then test yourself at the end of the day and then do one day using CASTT and test yourself at the end as well.

Which worked best for you?

....

....

One thing we've noticed is that pupils using the CASTT method generally say that it's much harder work than some of the other methods they have used – but it gets much more done. So expect to feel tired!

17. Vision Activity: Setting a Personal Best

You've probably heard of setting a personal best (PB) before. It's a term often used in the sporting world to explain when an athlete records their best ever time. It's something most athletes are always striving for – to push beyond a time or distance they've achieved before in an event. Quite often the goal is just to beat their last time or distance by a fraction of a second or a centimetre. The gains are usually small but make a big difference.

Professor Andrew Martin (2011) at the University of Sydney has used this strategy with pupils and found that it can make a big difference to academic performance.

So how does it work?

There are three important things about PBs. First, they are personal. That means *you* have to decide what the target is going to be. You can ask your teacher for advice, but ultimately it's about you deciding what you'd like to go for.

Second, you need to be specific. You can't set a target that isn't specific or you won't know when you've achieved a PB. So, it might be that you set a PB for specific homework, perhaps a percentage grade that you want to achieve that's better than you've had before.

Third, you need just the right level of challenge. This means pushing yourself out of your comfort zone (see the diagram below) and into your learning zone. Be careful not to push yourself into the panic zone. You want a PB that will stretch you but it must be achievable. You can always go for another PB once you've achieved this new level.

Getting the level of challenge right

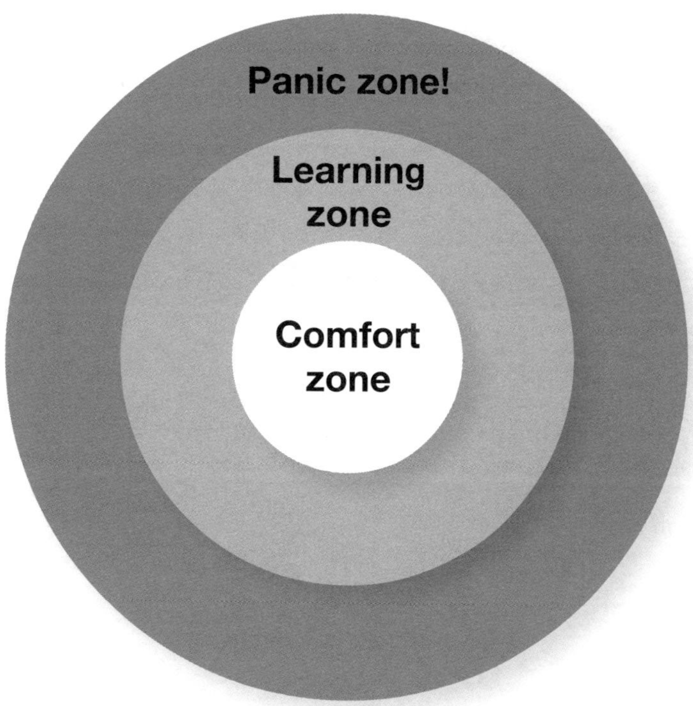

Finally, use the table below to set your PB. An example has been done for you.

Challenge (What's the goal?)	Current score (What's the best score you've achieved?)	PB target (What's the target for your new PB?)
To get my best ever score in a GCSE maths paper	67%	70%
....		
....		

Final Thoughts

When you set PBs there's always a point at which you hit a plateau. At this stage it can seem hard to make any progress. When you get to this point it's worth taking very small steps to help you progress. Remember, 1% gains over a period of time can have a significant effect.

Next time you hit a sticking point ask yourself the following questions:

Is it my knowledge of the content? Where are the gaps?

....

....

....

Is it my academic skills? Do I need to speak to my teacher for guidance?

....

....

....

Is it my mindset? Am I working on the things I know rather than the things I don't? How am I responding to feedback?

....

....

....

18. Vision Activity: Success Leaves Clues

Who's already done what you want to do?

Jim Rohn said that 'success leaves clues'. What he meant by this is that you can learn from other people who have already done what you'd like to do. There are millions of pupils who have already taken their GCSEs and millions of these pupils will have done really well. You'll probably find these pupils have some very good advice. It's crazy that we don't spend more time learning from people who have already been through what we would like to do and learning from their mistakes. The message is that we don't have to make the same mistakes!

So what did they do?

This activity involves you speaking to a pupil who has already done well in their GCSEs and maybe some pupils who didn't. This might be something that your teacher can arrange for you or you might be able to ask a friend's older brother or sister.

You'll need about fifteen minutes to do this activity. It might feel a bit awkward, but just think of yourself as a journalist trying to find out a story of success. You'll need a pen, paper and maybe a copy of the questions below. When you start the conversation, it will be worth writing down the answers or recording the conversation on your phone so you can listen to it later.

You could start the conversation by asking some of the following questions:

» What is your dream job?

» What obstacles do you think you may have to overcome while at school?

» What do you hope to achieve by completing your A levels/BTEC or apprenticeship?

» How many hours a week of independent study do you do for your GCSEs?

» Describe a typical hour of your revision.

» In an average week how many hours do you spend on homework?

» How do you decide what you need to revise?

» What do you do with work you get back?

» If you do past paper questions do you ever self-mark them?

» What advice would you give your Year 10 self when first starting your GCSEs?

» What revision materials do you use/produce?

» What do you do when you encounter a problem?

» How do you respond to setbacks?

» What is your response to a poor grade in a test or homework?

When you've finished the interview (it would be useful to do a few), identify what you think are the key points and write them in the table below. Try to get ten points for each column and then keep this visible in your study area at home.

What do successful pupils do?	What do pupils who haven't been successful do?
....	....
....	....
....	....
....	....
....	....
....	....
....	....
....	....
....	....
....	....

Final Thoughts

This is also a great technique to use with adults in the area you would like to work. Could you interview some people in your chosen career (if you have one), or could you interview some university students on the course you'd like to go on?

You could start by asking them about their study habits and then move on to questions that are more specific to their career, such as:

» Why did you choose your career?

» What do you love about it?

» What don't you like?

» What advice would you give someone just starting?

» What advice would you give someone my age?

January Activities

Just like September, January is one of those turning points in a year. The break gives us an opportunity to refocus, and to figure out what we want from the year ahead. We know there are only five months left, and that we're in complete control of what those summer results are going to look like, no matter what anyone else might tell us. This month's activities try to help you figure out what success looks like, so that you can remind yourself why you're doing this, and where it's going to take you. We've also focused on feedback this month – chances are you'll be collecting your mock exam results. If you're anything like most people, there will be results you're not happy with. Feedback becomes crucial in teaching you how to improve, yet sometimes we ignore it because we're angry or afraid.

19. Vision Activity: Five Roads

In this simple activity, all you need to do is imagine yourself at a crossroads with five possible ways forward. Each way forward represents a possible choice for you. The aim of this activity is to make those possible choices clearer. That way you can objectively review your options, which is the first step in making a good decision. Don't feel a decision has to be made yet – it doesn't. But knowing what options are in play is always helpful.

Use the image below to think about what might lie at the end of each road, and scribble some notes at the tip of each road. Make the notes as detailed as you can.

You might need to spend some time thinking about these. And it might be a good idea to begin by putting two or three options at the end of each road, and coming back to add more or cross others off as your preferences become clearer.

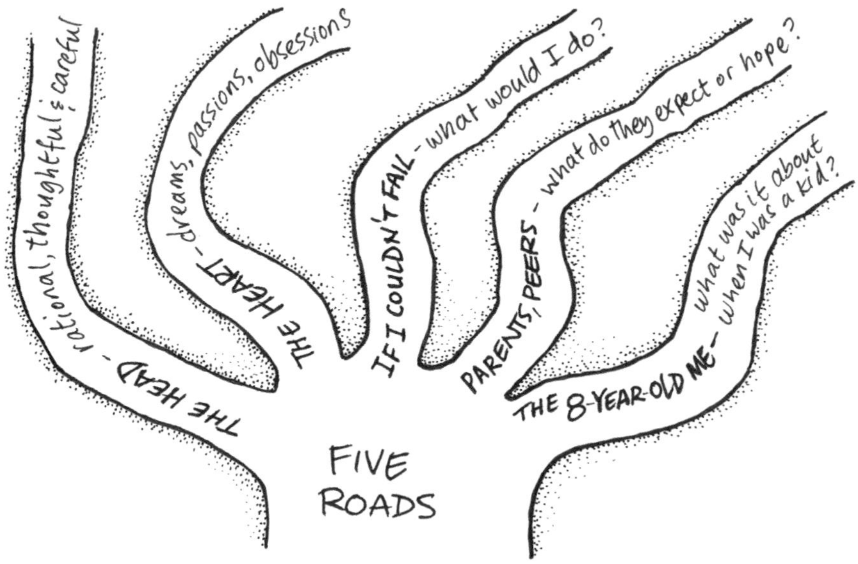

The head. Here, you put the choices that occur to you when you think rationally. This is the careful and thoughtful road. There will be low risk on this road – it's safe and certain. It might not be your most exciting road forward, though!

. . . .

. . . .

. . . .

. . . .

. . . .

The heart. This road is about wholeheartedly pursuing your passions; the stuff that makes you excited and that you would willingly spend time on doing for free. This might be a riskier road, with greater levels of uncertainty, but you'll be fired-up as well as slightly fearful as you travel it!

. . . .

. . . .

. . . .

. . . .

. . . .

If I couldn't fail. At the end of this imaginary road is guaranteed success in something. It will be a hard road to travel, and there may be tough times but it will, 100%, end in success. In other words: if you knew you couldn't fail at something, what would you choose to do?

. . . .

. . . .

. . . .

. . . .

. . . .

Parents, peers. Here, you consider what others are expecting of you. You may be surrounded by people with strong opinions; teachers, tutors, parents and extended family all telling you that you have to pursue something, or that you're a natural at something. You might, or might not, agree with them. Make a note of all the things you feel a pressure to pursue here.

. . . .

. . . .

. . . .

. . . .

. . . .

The 8-year-old me. If you'd done this activity in primary school, what would you have said you wanted to do in the future? Often, we find elements of our early passions still exist today – you might write something down here and suddenly remember a passion that you've forgotten, or forced yourself to ignore. Maybe it's time to revisit it. Maybe there are just parts of it that are still relevant today.

. . . .

. . . .

. . . .

. . . .

. . . .

Once you've got some ideas scribbled at the end of each road, let these ideas and thoughts develop for a few days. Consider returning to this activity more than once as the year goes on, adjusting your responses.

Final Thoughts

Don't feel you need to make a decision yet. Just knowing the possible ways forward puts you in a strong position. And when you travel a road, it doesn't mean you can never return to try another. You can!

20. Vision Activity: The Ten-Year Grid

We've based this activity on one proposed by Alison and David Price in their book *Psychology of Success: A Practical Guide* (2011), which we thoroughly recommend! Have a look at the grid below. It's a 20 x 26 grid with 520 little boxes in it. Each box represents a week of your life for the next ten years.

Now ask yourself what you want your life to be like in ten years' time. You don't have to be super-specific. Try to make notes under the following headings:

» A job that involves …

» Places I've enjoyed visiting, including …

» Friends and family I value because they …

» A lifestyle that allows me to …

This grid represents the weeks you've got to achieve all that.

Looking at it this way, ten years doesn't seem quite as much time. And it gets more alarming … Before you begin, shade out the following:

» Sleep: six full columns. Assuming just under eight hours a night, that's all the time in the next ten years that you'll be asleep – about 33% of the time!

» Leisure and 'trapped time': five full columns. We've gone to the Office for National Statistics for this one. After analysing lifestyles, they conclude that we spend about 6% of our time during mealtimes, about 11% of our time watching TV, 6% of our time travelling from one place to another and 2% of our time on 'personal care' (brushing teeth, make-up, shaving, etc.). That's about 25% of the next ten years you'll be using up.

So, in total you have to clear eleven of the twenty columns. That's over half your time!

Now how many weeks have you got left to build that life for yourself? 234. And that's assuming you want it to happen in ten years; secretly, you might really want it sooner. And there are other things that you haven't shaded off – school, family time and other commitments that remove blocks from the grid.

The conclusion: whatever it is you want to achieve, if you want it soon, *you need to get started*. What immediate actions could get your project underway? Make a note of the kind of things that could get you up and running here:

. . . .

. . . .

. . . .

. . . .

. . . .

The Power of Negative Visualisation

Think about your vision for a life ten years from now. Crazy as it sounds, the chances are that many of the obstacles you'll need to overcome won't come from external circumstances. They will come from *you*. You'll put obstacles in the way of your own potential happiness. In *Rethinking Positive Thinking* (2014), the psychologist Gabrielle Oettingen argues that we all have this tendency to sabotage our own success. But by confronting the obstacles we put in our own way – by visualising them blocking our progress – we get better at removing them.

Use the spaces below to try to tackle two questions:

Is there a part of your personality that might compromise your potential success?

Sometimes I can be …

. . . .

. . . .

What are the obstacles you might actually put in your own way?

Sometimes I have a tendency to …

. . . .

Now, imagine that, for one of the reasons you've thought about, you take no action towards your goal.

» Let's imagine you've just visualised an exciting life for yourself ten years from now, put this book down, and you've found, after a busy week, that you've taken no action. Shade out one week of your grid.

» Now imagine another month has passed – a busy month with lots going on – and you still haven't managed to get started. Shade out four more of your boxes. As you do this, try to put yourself in the shoes of the future you. With a month gone by, how is this feeling?

» What if Christmas comes around and you haven't been able to find the time or energy to take any action? That's three months. Shade out twelve of your boxes. Again, try to connect with the feelings you might experience if this really happens.

» A whole year is two full columns. Visualise a year having passed and, for whatever reason, you haven't yet managed to take any action. Scratch two columns. How would you be feeling if that really did happen?

» Now look further ahead. How will you feel if three years on – that's six full columns – you haven't done anything?

This negative visualisation might help you. Whenever time passes without you taking action, return to this grid and watch the weeks disappearing.

Then get yourself back on track!

Final Thoughts

Some pupils we work with subdivide the weeks ahead and set mini-goals. It often seems to work really well. Take a column – the equivalent of half a year – and set a goal for that six months. It can be smaller, more manageable, but a crucial step forward. Record it below:

A six month mini-goal

By . . . . (insert date) I will have . . . . (insert commitment)

If it works, you might want to build in some others too:

By . . . . (insert date) I will have . . . . (insert commitment)

By . . . . (insert date) I will have . . . . (insert commitment)

By . . . . (insert date) I will have . . . . (insert commitment)

By . . . . (insert date) I will have . . . . (insert commitment)

By . . . . (insert date) I will have . . . . (insert commitment)

21. Attitude Activity: The Battery

Dr Steve Bull was the England and Wales cricket team's psychologist for seventeen years, working with players who experienced huge pressure to perform day in, day out. As a result, he has developed a series of interesting tools for boosting people's confidence in their own ability. In his book, *The Game Plan* (2006, p. 33), Bull says, 'It seems to be a human frailty that we are programmed to focus on failure and disappointment far more than on success and accomplishment. We find it very easy to recall those disastrous days when everything went wrong.' He goes on to say that 'When we are faced with a similar challenge, our brains are quick to recall the previous catastrophe.' He then concludes that 'the cycle must be broken, and the most effective way of doing this is to actively reconnect your mind with previous accomplishments'. Dr Bull worked with cricketers, asking them to record their previous successes, and saw their confidence rocket and their performances improve as a result.

Bull uses mountain peaks as his confidence metaphor, but we prefer the image of a phone battery. We like the idea of a battery because confidence in your ability gives you energy. It charges you up and fills you with strength and belief. You can keep your battery topped up by recalling those times when things went brilliantly and you really achieved what you were capable of.

You have five energy slots to fill. Your job is to fill each slot above with a brief description of a time when you performed really well and achieved something you are pleased with or proud of. When you're feeling low, you can return to your battery, read the information there and feel yourself recharge with positivity and purpose.

But what do you write in the five slots? Try using the following as guidelines:

» Times when you supported or helped someone perform better or taught them something.

» Times when your family members valued you for doing the right thing, making a good decision or doing a good turn.

» Times when you worked in a team, adding value to that team.

» Times when you did something you felt scared about, facing down your fear.

» Times when you performed well in a test or a homework and got a grade/score you were pleased with.

» Times when you made a difficult decision.

» Times when your strengths, skills and talents meant you did a good job.

» Times you've been rewarded – either verbally through someone saying thank you, or via a letter home, a certificate or an award.

Go back as far as you can. A well-charged confidence battery draws on achievements from all areas of your life and from all times of your life, so don't limit yourself to school or this academic year. You've been doing good work for a long time now – think hard to recall it all!

Final Thoughts

If you're feeling low, a natural response to a task like this might be – 'I can't think of anything.' We've worked with lots of pupils who've responded this way. We've also responded this way ourselves when we've felt down about our situation or circumstances.

Here's some advice for when your inner critic – that negative voice we all sometimes have inside us – gets too noisy and confident:

Kill all comparisons. Let your negative voice say what it wants for a few minutes, but all comparisons are banned. If it tries telling you, 'You're not as good as …' – shut it down. It's called 'impostor syndrome', where you feel you are a fraud. 'I don't deserve to be here' or 'Others are cleverer than me' are common feelings and messages. Refuse to accept the voice if it tries any comparisons like these.

Use the space below to design a response to your inner critic when it gets like this. A quick, two or three sentence answer which stops it in its tracks:

. . . .

. . . .

. . . .

. . . .

. . . .

Challenge your inner critic with data. Your SATs scores. Your reports from Year 7, 8 or 9. The last decent grade you got on a piece of work. Or challenge your negative voice with a demand. 'Well if you think that, what should I do about it? Got any ideas?'

Use this space to plan a response that covers these two bases – drawing on data, and challenging the negative voice directly:

. . . .

. . . .

. . . .

. . . .

. . . .

22. Systems Activity: The Bottom Left

Sometimes the number of jobs you have to do can be overwhelming. Teachers are making demands from all angles and it's difficult to know where to start. The trouble with listing jobs is that a list doesn't allow you to see the bigger picture; you can't assess the progress of whole projects, you can only pick off small individual tasks.

Using a matrix or a grid helps you to assess the status of entire subjects. And once you've got a good sense of how an entire subject is going, you can use your time much more effectively, targeting your energy where it's most needed.

Put every subject you study onto this grid:

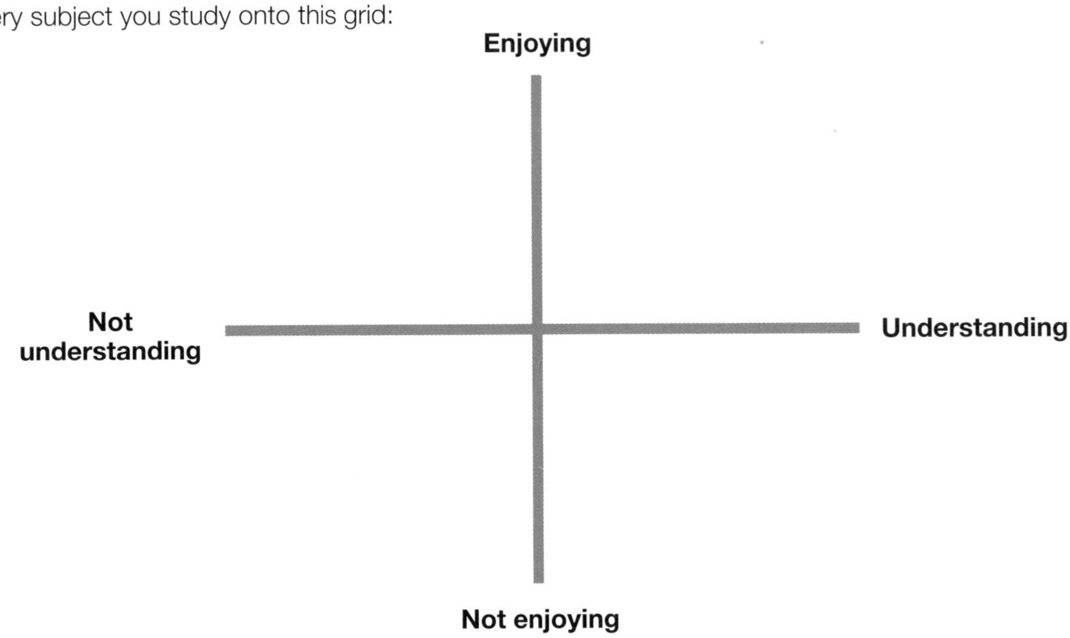

Once you've made these decisions and placed these projects as dots or crosses on the grid, make notes under each dot explaining the reasons why you've positioned it there. Then have a look at the projects in the bottom left of the grid.

The Terror of the Bottom Left!

Many pupils will subconsciously avoid the subjects in the bottom left because even the thought of them feels uncomfortable. They might lower the standards they expect of themselves in those subjects, work less hard at them or try to ignore them altogether. But they're not going to go away. By spending some time on them now you could avoid a real crisis later on in the year.

Let's examine the subjects closest to – or in – the bottom left quadrant. We've given you enough space here to deal with three or four problem subjects! For each of your bottom left subjects make a note of:

» One task you could do that will push the dot further to the right.

» One task you could do that will push the dot further upwards.

. . . .

. . . .

. . . .

. . . .

It might be speaking to a teacher, borrowing some missing work, attending an after-school class, speaking to a pupil who's better at it than you, finishing reading a textbook or redoing a rushed piece of homework. Consider the fourteen suggestions in Looking Under the Rocks (page 33) for inspiration!

Good prioritisation means knowing *why you're doing what you're doing*. This task will help you to focus on your weaknesses.

Final Thoughts

Here's the problem with to-do lists. No matter how you prioritise your list, all the tasks there still take up the same amount of physical space (a line of A4 paper), and so end up taking the same amount of mental space.

But not all tasks are equally important.

Any associated with subjects that are currently in the top right quadrant, where you're understanding and enjoying the work, are a little less important than the tasks associated with the bottom left.

Have a look at the tasks you've got for subjects in the top right quadrant. Is there any way you can complete these tasks more quickly and efficiently? Any small corners you can cut? Any favours you can call in or people you can ask for help? (See Network Audits, page 31 for more on this …) Your aim is to buy yourself some time by working super-efficiently in the subjects that are currently going well.

Scribble some possible ideas here:

. . . .

. . . .

. . . .

. . . .

Now you've potentially saved yourself some time, which task in the bottom left quadrant needs the most work?

. . . .

Use this saved time to get started on it now!

23. Attitude Activity: Managing Reactions to Feedback

Our response to getting feedback can vary considerably. Some people are hungry for feedback and want to know how they can improve; others avoid feedback like the plague and take it personally. If you want to get good grades at GCSE you are going to have to get comfortable with feedback. Steve Bull, in his brilliant book *The Game Plan* (2006, p. 125), has developed an acronym, SADRAA, to help you with the process. He suggests that when you get feedback you might not be happy with, you should work through three stages: the red zone, the blue zone and the green zone.

The table below explains the zones. Low performing pupils can sometimes get caught up in the red zone and some might never leave. You might know people like this! It's fine to have these initial emotions, of course, but then you must push through the next two stages.

The red zone Emotions	**S**hock	Wow – I did not expect that! I'm really surprised by those comments.
	Anger	How dare they say that! That teacher has never liked me. Wait till I get my own back.
	Denial	I'm not like that at all. That's totally wrong.
The blue zone Thinking	**R**ationalisation	OK, maybe it seems true from their perspective. But the reason they think that is because they don't know what kind of pressure I'm under. Anyway, that's the way I am and why should I change? And even if I wanted to, how could I?
The green zone Behaviour	**A**cceptance	OK, maybe I need to change something. Maybe I could look at a few different ways of doing things to see if they improve matters.
	Action	Right, what do I need to do?

The next time that you have some feedback that you might not be happy with, use the table below to either record your own thoughts or check in with your emotional response to the criticism and see which zone you're in. Then look ahead to the next zone and see what kind of thoughts you might try to have to move yourself through the process more quickly. Ultimately, you'll be much happier if you avoid getting stuck in the red or blue zone!

It might be tricky to get to the green zone, so feel free to leave it a day or so – maybe longer – before completing the final box or considering the ideas you see there.

The zones	Your thoughts ...
The red zone Emotions	....

The zones	Your thoughts ...
The blue zone Thinking	....
The green zone Behaviour	....

Final Thoughts

One way to fully understand Bull's model is to watch other people responding to feedback. Watch for feedback after a sporting fixture, and see how players react. Watch out for how your parents describe taking feedback, or even your teachers. Most of all, watch for how your friends talk about feedback. If you're surrounded by people who can't take feedback, it makes it harder to learn how to handle it well.

Austin Kleon (2014, pp. 134–136), a writer and artist, warns us to make sure we have positive friends. He calls negative friends 'vampires'. Kleon advises that, 'if, after hanging out with someone you feel worn out and depleted, that person is a vampire. If, after hanging out with someone you still feel full of energy, that person is not a vampire.'

It's worth thinking about the five people you spend most time with, and asking yourself five questions about them ...

1. Are they positive people?
2. Do they enjoy their lives?
3. Are they a good influence?
4. Have they helped you through problems?
5. Do they make you feel good about yourself, and about life?

....

....

....

....

....

February Activities

Whatever news has come in January, February is the month to respond to it. This is the month to establish some new habits. Forget about trying to break old habits, simply focus on starting some new ones. Beginning something is a much more positive experience than trying to stop something, so make February your month for starting a habit. This month's activities give you some ideas for starting positive study habits that could well stay with you until the summer. We've also given you advice on how to begin rescuing subjects that are falling behind, and being courageous enough to spend time working on weaknesses.

24. Effort Activity: The Effort Thermometer

If you want to be successful at anything you're going to have to put the work in – it's that simple.

There are a number of people who think that their talent is average, but their work ethic separates them from the rest. The actor Will Smith is a great example of someone who claims he doesn't have much talent and it's his work ethic that separates him from the rest. Here's what he says about hard work:

> *The only thing that I see that is distinctly different about me is I'm not afraid to die on a treadmill. I will not be out-worked, period. You might have more talent than me, you might be smarter than me, you might be sexier than me, you might be all of those things – you got it on me in nine categories. But if we get on the treadmill together, there's two things: you're getting off first or I'm going to die. It's really that simple, right?*

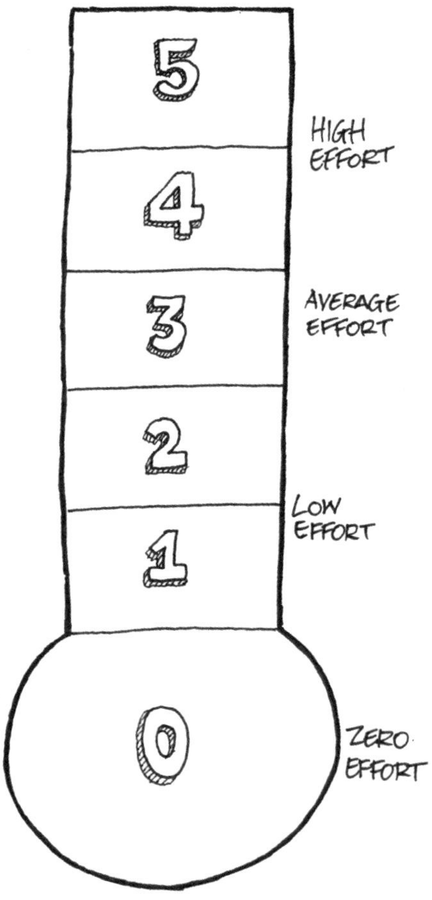

The effort thermometer is a way of getting you to keep track of how hard you're working. The first thing you have to decide is what are high levels of effort.

It might be best if you do this activity with your tutor group or ask a few friends for their thoughts. Next to 'high effort' write down what the high effort pupils are doing. (We've done this activity a number of times before. Here are the kinds of things we often get back: does ten hours of revision each week, always stays focused in class, works hard in every lesson, does additional work on top of homework, asks teachers questions to fix misunderstandings, attends lunchtime sessions or after-school catch-ups.)

Next, you then need to do the same for average effort and low effort pupils. How are the behaviours here different?

Now it's time to rate yourself. Be honest – no one else is ever going to see this. Where would you put yourself on the scale – low, average or high?

Once you've made your decision, answer the following questions:

1. Are you working hard enough yet? ....

2. Are you *reactive* (responding to teacher instruction only) or *proactive* (sorting things out yourself, setting yourself extra work, taking responsibility for your own progress)? Place a cross on the line below to represent where you think you might be:

Reactive ←————————————→ Proactive

Why have you made this decision? Make a note of the evidence:

....

3. What things could you change? How could you push the cross further to the right? Try thinking of four steps forward:

....

....

....

....

4. Make a note of three or four pupils who are working harder than you. What are they doing?

....

....

....

5. Have you got the balance right between work and rest? What adjustments could you make?

....

....

....

Repeat this activity every term: as you progress through the year, the amount of effort you need to put in changes.

Final Thoughts

Try setting short-term goals to help you boost your effort. Instead of thinking 'This is how hard I'm going to have to work for the rest of the year!', which can be a daunting prospect, you might instead set yourself a date where you take a mini-break. Try working harder for three or four days before rewarding yourself. Then work for five days at a new level of effort. Then eight or nine. Try for longer and longer periods, building in breaks.

These mini-breaks help break up the time ahead of you and keep you motivated.

25. Effort Activity: Packing My Bags

Often, our perception of our own effort is inaccurate. We frequently judge it by the people we surround ourselves with. So, if someone asked you how hard you are working, you might think about your three closest friends, figure out how you're doing compared to them and then give an answer. This is fine if all your friends are really hard working. If not, you might be kidding yourself that you're doing enough work.

It can be useful to do a checklist to review how hard you are working and see if you need to make any changes.

Have a go. First, you need to look at the behaviours listed below and then decide if this is something you do consistently (at least once every week), sometimes (at least every three weeks to a month) or rarely (once a term or even never). Then you have to decide whether you think this is a development need (something you should improve). If you think that it's something you should consider as a development need, your final task is to prioritise it as either high, medium or low, depending on how you think it will impact your performance.

Behaviour	Demonstrated consistently/ sometimes/rarely	Development need: high/ medium/low
I always hand my homework in on time. I leave things until the last minute. I do the minimum amount of work I can get away with. I hand in extra exam work for marking. In most classes my main goal is to do the minimum needed so I don't have to work very hard. I work hard at home. I do ten hours a week of independent study at home.		

The next step is to decide what you are happy with and what you aren't happy with.

This activity uses the analogy of packing your bags for a holiday. Imagine you're leaving the present you behind and moving to a new you. There are going to be some things that you want to take with you – elements of your current habits and work practices that you really like – and some things that you will definitely want to leave behind – things that annoy you about yourself or end up causing you stress and anxiety.

Use the table below and decide what you need to improve (put those in the 'pack to take' column) and what you need to leave behind.

Pack to take	Leave behind

Pack to take	Leave behind

Finally, you need to decide on a date – that is, the date you're leaving behind all the stuff you don't want to be part of your school life (everything you've put in the right-hand column).

Give yourself a few days. You'll need to be mentally ready to count down to this date and look forward to it.

A tip: we've found it's good to make it a Thursday or Friday. It'll be tiring being the new you. Start on a Monday and by Wednesday you'll be exhausted! We've found that pupils have more success when they give themselves a day or two of their new self before a weekend comes along to save them …

Date to change:

. . . .

Final Thoughts

Sometimes, after setting a date, a pupil has a setback. They forget their new pattern of behaviour just for a day, and things go wrong. When that happens, it's tempting to abandon the whole plan. Don't do that! If something goes wrong and you slip, just put it behind you, and commit to starting again the following day. Sometimes there are two or three false starts before you crack it!

26. Effort Activity: Twenty-Five Minute Sprints

There's a very famous book by Italian entrepreneur and author Francesco Cirillo called *The Pomodoro Technique*. Pomodoro is Italian for tomato. (The tomato in question is one of those novelty kitchen timers, not a real one!) We'll come back to the tomato in a bit.

In his book, Cirillo argues that we can generate lots of energy and effort by working in short bursts, even on long tasks that we don't feel motivated to do. Think of all the tasks you've got to do that you just can't bear to begin – there might be revision notes, essays to write, jumbled notes to file away or a piece of coursework to start.

Choose one that's become a bit of a nightmare for you – that's hanging over your head and you just don't want to do. Make a note of it here:

. . . .

Step 1

Now for the tomato. By which we mean getting hold of either a kitchen timer (needless to say, it doesn't have to be shaped like anything in particular!) or the timer on your phone.

Find somewhere quiet. Arrange the things you need to begin. You're going to do a twenty-five minute sprint. It's important to tell yourself this: *twenty-five minutes – that's all*. You're allowed no distractions whatsoever in that twenty-five minutes. Don't worry. You can be back on social media in twenty-five minutes' time, checking updates and messages. Now start the timer and go!

Step 2

Congratulations! You've got that nightmare task started. All of a sudden, this job is going to seem less frightening. You'll be able to come back to it. Some suggestions for messing around with the Pomodoro Technique:

1. The Quick Sprint: try twenty-five minutes on, twenty-five minutes off, twenty-five minutes on. It takes one hour and fifteen minutes in total, and you can do it at a regular time each night after school.
2. The Serious Sprint: try twenty-five minutes on, five minutes off, twenty-five minutes on, five minutes off, twenty-five minutes on. It takes about one hour and thirty minutes, and is a useful technique for really attacking a difficult piece of work.
3. Try measuring tasks in sprints. How many will it take? This way, you'll develop a sense of how you work, and you can begin picking off scary tasks more quickly and easily.
4. Try using sprints to review work. Suddenly you'll find yourself ahead and on top of things. It's a great feeling!

Setting Up a Quick Sprint

Preparation	25 minutes on!	25 minutes off	25 minutes on!
» Find somewhere quiet. » Gather everything you need. » Put phone on airplane settings. » Bring up timer, set countdown and alarm. » Tell yourself: 'Just 25 minutes. That's all.'	» Go! » Imagine it's an exam. » Stay intense, keep going.	» Set timer and countdown. » Enjoy yourself.	» Tell yourself: 'Just one last 25 minute blast. That's all.' » Put phone back on airplane settings. » Return to the task. » Go!

Final Thoughts

One Quick Sprint per day for a week is nearly six hours' independent work per week.

One Serious Sprint per day is nearly ten hours' independent work per week.

Try using a Mission and Medal weekly planner to scope out a week with:

» six hours' independent learning

» ten hours' independent learning

» fifteen hours' independent learning

	Before school (early morning – 7am–8.30am)	During school (morning and early afternoon – 9am–3pm)	After school (twilight – 4pm–5.30pm)	Evening (7pm–9.30pm)
Monday				
Mission:				
Medal:				
Tuesday				
Mission:				
Medal:				
Wednesday				
Mission:				
BONUS medal:				
Thursday				
Mission:				
Medal:				
Friday				
Saturday				
Sunday				
Mission:				
BONUS medal:				

27. Practice Activity: The Nine-Box Grid

Before you really begin to attack your revision, you need to be able to actively recast the information you need to learn. That means rewriting or reorganising your class notes into something you have built yourself – something you've processed and created. No passive reading and highlighting of notes here – just active, engaged rewriting!

You don't want to be spending too much of your time on this – we recommend about 50% of your revision time should be recasting notes – but it's a crucial step.

One way to do it that we've really enjoyed is the nine-box grid. (An A level physics pupil taught us this one. He ended up at Oxford so we know it works!) And here's the best bit: all you'll need is a sheet of A4 paper.

Place the paper in front of you – orient it landscape – and fold it into thirds, like this:

Then, with it folded, do it again the other way so that when you open up you've got nine squares:

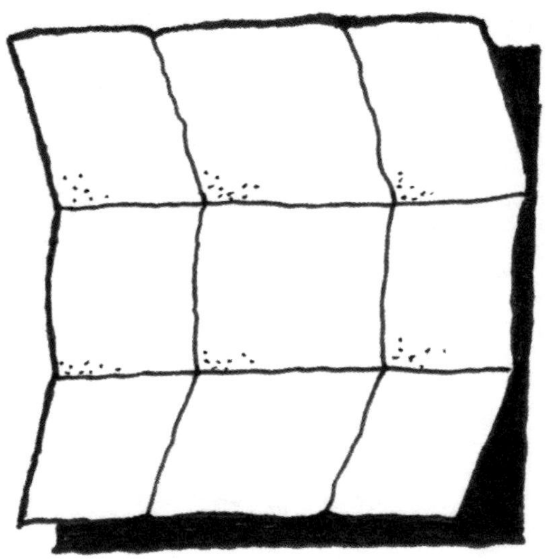

There are three steps to filling in the grid:

1. Your challenge is to summarise an entire topic (or, if you're feeling brave, an entire course) in nine boxes. First, you need to read through your notes on the topic/course and decide what your nine boxes are. Ask yourself: what are the nine key subsections? Ask teachers to suggest nine. Work with friends to identify the nine. Go through exam papers to see if they help you decide on the nine.

Subject or topic:

. . . .

Nine possible topic areas:

....

....

....

....

....

....

....

....

....

2. Once you've got the nine subsections, you need to find a way to summarise your notes using just the little boxes on the grid. You can't use any additional space. Don't try to write so small you can't read it! Use diagrams, pictures, mind-maps or other graphic organisers to condense your information. Do what you have to, but get it all down in the nine little boxes. Then photograph it in case it gets lost!
3. Now read through the whole grid and, on the other side, draw up a list of key concepts, ideas and vocabulary you're going to need to master. That's it. An entire course or topic on one sheet of paper.

Once you've got your nine-box grid, you're ready to attempt exam questions. You'll see other pupils laboriously rereading their notes or copying out the entire course in their lucky pen – but ignore them. You've got the content nailed on one sheet!

Final Thoughts

Remember, even if you're the greatest builder of nine-box grids the world has ever seen, you still need to be moving on to other revision activities – the ones that will test your skills and get you used to performing confidently under exam conditions.

We'd recommend you do two things next:

Check your responses to the revision questionnaire, and move onto activities in the S and F sections of the questionnaire now that you've mastered C – the content bit.

Try using your nine-box grid as the basis of another activity in this book: It's Time to Teach, aka CASTT. If you've got a nine-box grid done, you've already completed the C and A of CASTT! Check out what to do next on page 40.

28. Practice Activity: Will vs. Skill

If you ask most pupils what they spend most of their revision time on, if they are honest they will say revising things that they like doing. It's quite normal when you think about it. We all like to spend time on activities we feel comfortable or confident doing.

The problem can be that we're putting off things we feel uncomfortable with or don't like doing.

Everyone has heard of Usain Bolt – the world's fastest man to ever run 100 metres. He has an interesting way of approaching his training. He works out where his weak spots are and then spends most of his time training on them. For Bolt, that's the start of his 100 metres. He's a big guy and getting out of the blocks requires a lot of effort for him. He says he knows that it's his area of vulnerability. He's not great at it (he's 'low skill' when it comes to bursting from the blocks), and what's more, he doesn't particularly enjoy this aspect of his training (he is 'low will' in this area – that is, he has to force himself to do it, almost against his will). Despite these obstacles, Bolt spends a significant part of his training on this element because he knows that this is where he can improve the most.

The Will vs. Skill matrix is a useful way of helping you to identify where you need to spend your time practising. It's not just Bolt's idea; it was made popular in the *Tao of Coaching* by Max Landsberg. Let's see if it helps you like it helped Usain Bolt.

Step 1

Pick one of your subjects. Make a list of all the topic areas that you need to cover in your revision. If you've done a nine-box grid for the subject, this will be much easier …

....

....

....

....

....

....

Step 2

Next, put each of the topic areas into the grid below. You need to make two judgements about the topic area to place it correctly. First, how good at it are you (that's the level of skill)? Second, how keen on it are you (that's your level of will)?

» **High will/low skill.** Here you put the topics that you like doing but you are still developing your skills. For example, you might like research methods in sociology but you know that you need to develop your expertise.

» **High will/high skill.** Here list all the topics that you love doing and that you are good at.

» **Low will/low skill.** In this box write a list of the topics you don't like and you know that your skills need developing.

» **Low will/high skill.** This is an interesting box. It's the topics you might not be keen on but you are good at them.

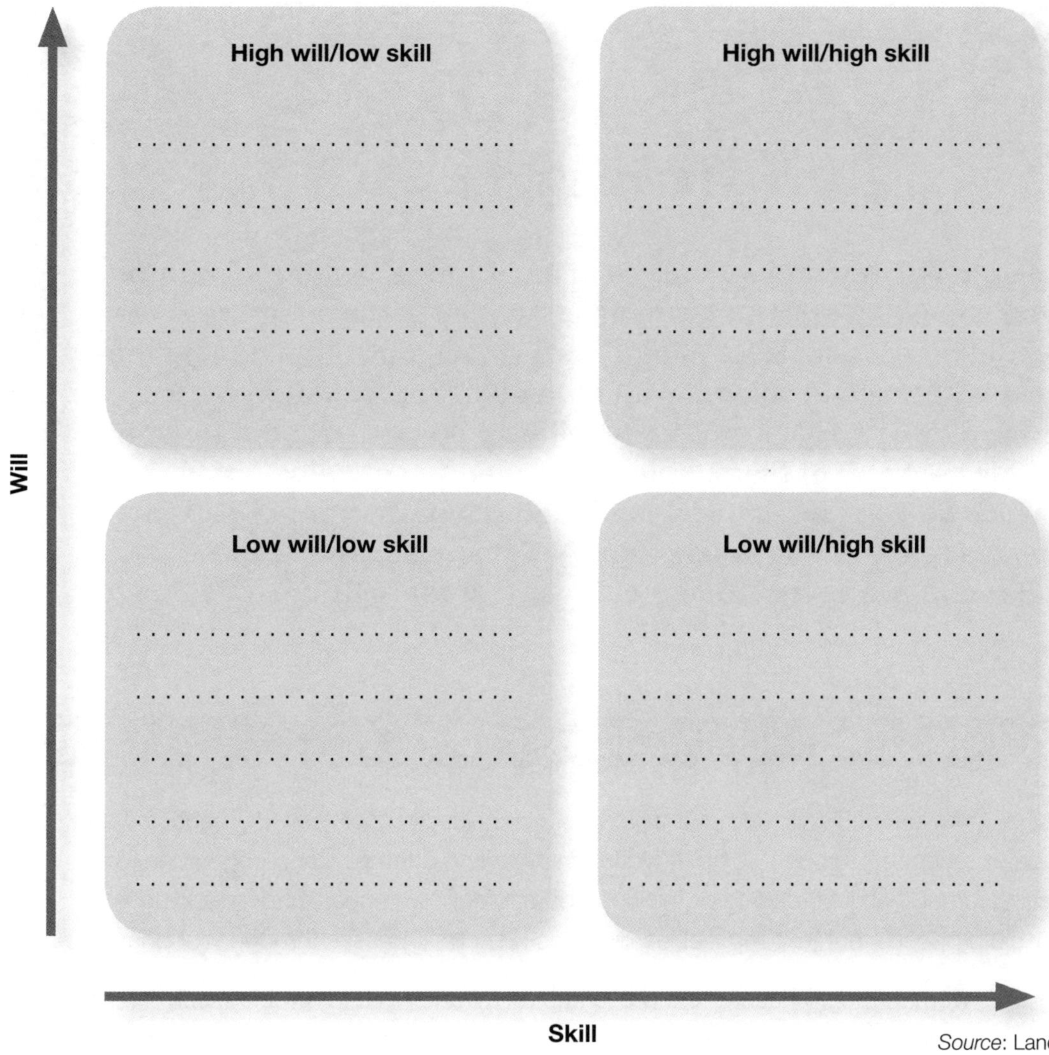

Source: Landsberg (2003), p. 55.

When you've added all the topics to the table, it's time for some reflection.

Where have you been spending most of your revision time? Is it time to tackle the low will/low skill box?

Final Thoughts

It's important to choose a high energy, positive time of day to tackle low will/low skill topics and subjects. If you had to choose a time of day when you feel most alert would it be:

- ❑ Early morning
- ❑ Late morning (pre-lunch)
- ❑ Early afternoon (post-lunch)
- ❑ Late afternoon (just after school)
- ❑ Evening

Now choose a day of the week when you've got some space and freedom at that time of day, and set aside an hour or two to tackle a low will/low skill topic or subject.

Finally, make sure you line up a great reward for getting the job done!

March Activities

The last three months of any project can be scary. But the last three months of something you've been working at *for five years* can feel even more momentous. Sometimes we feel like hiding from what's coming – hoping that somehow it'll never happen. Problems with study build up because we're pretending they don't exist. This month's activities help you get your head out of the sand and tackle a few of them. You might need to set aside some time with these activities so you can actively think about what's cropping up to stop you, and then plan a really effective solution. And because your revision is approaching full swing, we've included a couple of great revision activities too.

29. Attitude Activity: The Problem Solving Cycle

This activity is based on the work of David Kolb of the University of Leicester. Kolb's work suggests that we learn best through experience – through doing. If we take action and attempt a challenge (therefore experiencing something rather than just reading or thinking about it) our awareness, understanding and mastery increases. Kolb proposes that 'experiential learning', as he calls it, passes through four phases.

When we first saw Kolb's work, his four phases were presented as a framework for problem solving. It worked really well for us and we became hooked. We'll share what we learned with you here. You'll need to set aside thirty minutes to start with.

First, choose a problem you're battling with or a barrier you're facing. It might be to do with study habits, current performance, levels of energy or a subject-specific issue.

The problem or barrier: ____

The result of the problem: ____

Now break down the problem into the four stages of Kolb's problem solving cycle. Use the guidance below to inform you how to approach each stage.

4. Experiment with a course of action	**1. Explore the problem**
Key question: 'How did it go, and what have I learned?' You'll be in this phase for a week. Try one of your top three adjustments. As you go along, get a sense of how it is working. Persist with it, thinking about its impact on your learning. Then assess it at the end of the period. Discard, repeat or modify.	**Key question:** 'What is currently happening?' Stay here for ten minutes, assessing *the exact situation you are in*. Do not use judgemental or emotional language ('terrible', 'crap', 'nightmare'). Use facts and figures ('I'm on a grade E', 'My motivation is very low'). Dredge up every last bit of evidence you can find – grades, test scores, attendance, levels of effort and energy, feedback. Describe only – do not use 'because' yet; avoid justifying anything. Calmly list everything about your current situation.

3. Decide a course of action

Key question: 'What are my options?'

Stay here for ten minutes. Look back at what is happening and why. *Only focus on the things you can solve*. Calmly set aside things outside your control. Sift through your analysis of the problem and begin listing things you could do. Be uncritical; ignore the part of your brain saying, 'That's a terrible idea!' or 'How could that work? It's ridiculous!' and continue to list courses of action. Start with 'I could …' and go from there. When you're stuck, bring to mind everyone who could help – teachers, tutors, mentors, parents, family, friends.

When you've completed your list, choose your favourite three, then your top option.

2. Analyse the problem

Key question: 'Why is it happening?'

Stay here for ten minutes. List every single reason *why the problem is happening*. Make your list as long as possible, exploring yourself and your own actions, your attitudes and beliefs, the influence of those around you, your classrooms, lessons, work materials, the impact of external events, the impact of teachers and tutors and so on.

Calmly list everything, making sure nothing is missed. Do not bother yourself with solutions yet. Take your time.

4. Experiment with a course of action **Key question:** 'How did it go, and what have I learned?'	**1. Explore the problem** **Key question:** 'What is currently happening?' ....
3. Decide a course of action **Key question:** 'What are my options?'	**2. Analyse the problem** **Key question:** 'Why is it happening?' ....

Each of us apparently has a preference for one of these stages and might have a tendency to linger in it or even stay there as long as possible. We all know someone who endlessly talks about a problem without ever doing something about it. That person might feel most comfortable in stage 2 – analysing the problem. Other people you know might leap to a swift conclusion and do something straight away without properly thinking it through – perhaps they feel less comfortable in stages 1 and 2 and want to hurry on to stages 3 and 4.

For the cycle to work, stay in each quadrant for a good period of time, getting the most out of each stage.

The solutions you come up with will be better ones as a result!

Final Thoughts

Kolb's approach to problem solving is called root cause analysis – that is, a close examination of why a problem is occurring – what's at its root; or where it's growing from.

But there are other approaches to problem solving. Have a look at this short list, and see if alternative approaches might help you generate possible solutions too. There's a little space under each approach for you to scribble some initial ideas – maybe one of these will unlock your issue!

1. **Breaking Down.** One big problem might look too much to handle. But every big problem is composed of smaller problems. With this approach, you identify one or two smaller issues, and you try to fix those first.

....

....

....

2. **ODA.** Designed by a US Airforce colonel called John Boyd, this stands for observe, decide, act. A simple three-step problem solving approach that begins with closely studying a problem before choosing a way forward.

....

....

....

3. **Prove it!** Using this technique, you *try to prove the problem is impossible to solve*. Get as much evidence as you can to prove there's no way out. Wherever you can't prove it's impossible to solve, make a note of why. Here, apparently, lie the possible solutions.

....

....

....

30. Practice Activity: K-SPA

Chartered psychologist and university lecturer Alison Price is interested in the psychology of successful people. Having spent time researching and interviewing, she proposes an interesting model for the types of preparation people do before a breakthrough. These barrier-busting breakthroughs don't come overnight, Price argues – they're the result of careful planning, preparation and determined action.

But faced with a problem, it's normal to sometimes feel gloomy and defeated. It's really hard to know what great preparation should look like. How do we get past this? Where should we start? What should we do next?

We've had fun adapting Price's work to create the K-SPA model below. It suggests four things you should focus on in order to break through a barrier and become better at something. It's like a four-step plan to follow:

K = Knowledge. Things you need to *know more about* in order to break down the barrier.

S = Shopping. Things it would be *useful to have* to break down the barrier.

P = Practising. Things you *need to be better at* in order to break down the barrier.

A = Action. Things you could *do right now* to break down the barrier.

First, begin by identifying your barrier. You're capable of blasting it away in the next few weeks. Choose a barrier that is preventing you from improving; perhaps a problem you've identified using the previous activity (The Problem Solving Cycle).

The problem or barrier:

. . . .

. . . .

The result of the problem:

. . . .

. . . .

Now use the four headings to begin brainstorming solutions. Once you've got a whole bunch under each heading, your task is to choose the one that will have the highest impact, and commit to it. You should end up with four doable actions that you can now sequence!

Knowledge	Possible areas for research and learning: . . . .
	The one thing I'll study:
Shopping	Possible purchases: . . . .
	The one thing I'll buy:

Practising	Possible areas for practice:	....
	....	....
	....	....
	The one thing I'll practise:	
Action	Possible actions I could take straight away:	....
	....	....
	....	....
	The one thing I'll do now:	

The important thing here is to commit to the four actions. To maximise your chances of success, choose actions you know you can execute, and schedule them so you know when you should be taking that action.

If you're stuck or it didn't work, return to your list of possible actions and choose another!

Final Thoughts

This activity works a little like Looking Under the Rocks, aka Four Steps Forward (page 33) because it gives you four simple things to go and do. Remember you don't need to do them in order! Try this. **Place your four actions from hardest to do, to easiest to do**. Now complete them in this order:

Make **action one the second easiest**.

Action one: ....

By when? ....

Make **action two the third easiest**.

Action two: ....

By when? ....

Now give yourself a reward. You've done two of your four steps. Treat yourself!

Make **action three the easiest action** to do.

Action three: ....

By when? ....

Finish with **action four – the hardest of the lot**!

Action four: ....

By when? ....

31. Practice Activity: Spaced Practice

Studies show that snacking regularly on learning beats bingeing. In other words, rather than cram immediately before an exam, you can save time and energy by starting earlier and spacing out smaller sessions of practice and revision. You use your memory more this way. And as Benedict Carey says in his book *How We Learn* (2015, p. 40), 'using memory changes memory'. The more often something is recalled, the stronger the memory gets; a cycle of 'learn, forget, relearn, remember again' is strengthening your memory. A whole bunch of studies show that this process of spaced practice works way better than cramming. It also involves working for shorter periods rather than sitting down for epic sessions the night before an exam. That's a win-win.

But how do you space out practice? Well, that depends on how long it is before your exam. Since we're putting this activity in the March section of the book, we're going to build a programme of spaced practice that assumes three months until your exam, but if you're using this at another time of year, don't worry!

A study by academic researchers at the University of California San Diego (Cepeda et al., 2008) concluded the following about spacing:

Time to exam	Optimum study intervals
1 week	Every 1–2 days
1 month (4 weeks)	1 week
3 months (12 weeks)	2 weeks
6 months (26 weeks)	3 weeks
1 year (52 weeks)	1 month

Source: Summarised by Carey (2015), p. 77.

So, for our purposes, you need to be reviewing topics every two weeks, allowing them to fade in the gaps, then refreshing them when the next test comes along.

You don't necessarily have to do this for all your exams. Start by choosing a subject that you think needs a boost and plan out some spaced practice using the grid below. We've given some examples to help get you started.

Week	1	2	3	4	5	6	7	8	9	10	11	12
Topic A	Revise		Deep review		Deep review		Deep review		Quick review		Quick review	
Topic B		Revise		Deep review		Deep review		Deep review		Quick review		Quick review
Topic C												
Topic D												
Topic E												
Topic F												

Note: Revise – an initial study of the topic, summarising it; deep review – an in-depth revision session, re-remembering everything; quick review – a shorter, light touch review, checking memory.

One more thing: look out for what researchers call the 'fluency illusion' – that is, the tendency for us to be able to recall facts very quickly immediately after study. It might make you think, 'I've got this nailed. I can do it!' That might not be the case. Let it fall into your subconscious during the gap, then try to recall it again.

A little more detail:

Deep Reviews

These often involve a detailed, slow trawl of the information; going through it bit by bit, remembering everything and checking understanding, sometimes chasing down missing information or correcting errors. Aim for a whole topic in one sitting. You're building good, strong foundations.

Quick Reviews

These might involve something much speedier and lighter – you might be reading through, recapping, or best of all teaching the information you've pulled together in the deep review.

Final Thoughts

Imagine memory as a muscle, lifting things from your subconscious to your conscious, like a weightlifter hauling up weights.

Lifting things back into your conscious takes muscles. But sometimes we try to remember things – to lift them into the light – without practising lifting. No wonder we find it exhausting! Often pupils who haven't practised lifting enough say, 'I have a terrible memory,' or 'I can never remember anything.' What they mean is 'I haven't practised recalling things enough.'

And here's the good news – you can make lifting easier!

Have a go at this simple (and not very serious!) experiment. What follows are two lists of twenty words each.

List A is arranged alphabetically.

Study it for sixty seconds. Cover the words up and see how many you recall.

Then have a look at the words in list B, arranged thematically.

Study them for sixty seconds. Cover them up and see how many you can recall.

Now compare your two scores!

List A score: .... List B score: ....

Most people have a better result with list B than list A.* Why? Well, we've rigged the game a little. List B is the second list you've tried to memorise so you've had a little more practice. And list B is arranged thematically, so it gives you a better chance of recalling the words.

In conclusion then, regular recall from organised notes might well give you a better chance of success.

** If you scored higher on list A than B, you might consider skipping this activity and choosing another instead! We're all (slightly) different in the way we work and remember things …*

LIST A:

Amber
Anger
Bench
Butter dish
Cheese
Croissant
Danger
Delicious
Dracula
Football
Haircut
Hammer
Hedgerow
Jigsaw
Juice
Jupiter
Parliament
PIN
Shoes
Triumph

LIST B:

Green things	Bathroom items	Working breakfast	Mythical creatures
Apple	Toothbrush	Coffee	Unicorn
Leaves	Tap	Pastries	Dragon
Cactus	Mirror	Cornflakes	Ghost
Fields	Razor	Newspaper	Yeti
Envy	Soap	Commute	Zombie

32. Practice Activity: Test Yourself!

Dr Jennifer McGahan is a lecturer in psychology at Manchester Metropolitan University. Her research has focused on helping pupils to improve their memory, which is pretty useful for GCSE pupils. She shared this activity with us – many thanks, Jennifer. Over to you!

Taking a test does more than just assess your abilities; research has shown that it can also improve your memory for the information tested. Henry Roediger at Washington University has led the research in this area, now known as the 'testing effect'.

The term 'test' in this context refers to the act of retrieving information from your long-term memory. This can take many forms such as reciting facts about the Second World War aloud or completing a practice essay question. The test format is irrelevant; as long as you recall the information from memory, the rate at which you forget this information in the future is slowed down. This is in stark contrast to repeated study (reading over notes/highlighting text); when this technique is used information is forgotten much more quickly afterwards.

Despite huge amounts of research all showing the clear benefits of testing, most pupils prefer to revise for exams by reading information repeatedly. This is because the more you read something, the more familiar the content feels, resulting in a false sense of understanding and accomplishment. In contrast, testing yourself can feel challenging and frustrating, especially when you start to revise a new topic and it feels as though you are not recalling very much at all. Don't let this put you off: searching for the right answer (even unsuccessfully) strengthens the pathways in your brain for that information. Although it may feel counter-intuitive to test yourself, struggling is good for your brain and results in excellent learning in the end!

Remember that *all* exams require you to recall information; it is unlikely that an exam will test you on how well you can read text over and over again. Every time you test yourself you are reinforcing the connections in your brain in an outward direction, making them increasingly accessible for when you need it most – in an exam!

Top tips for testing yourself:

» Create elaborate links between new information and existing knowledge. This will make it easier to cue yourself during tests.

» Mind-maps are a great way of testing yourself. Close your books and scribble down everything you can remember. Number the points to track your progress.

» Feedback is essential when testing yourself to make sure that you do not learn any mistakes you may have made. This is especially important if you are using multiple choice tests as the right and wrong answers can be very similar.

How to Build a Killer Test

Step 1: Select a topic for study. Generate some headings and subheadings yourself that will act as cues.

Subject:	**Topic:** ....
Subheading 1:	Key information: ....
Subheading 2:	Key information: ....

Subject:	Topic: . . . .
Subheading 3:	Key information: . . . .
Subheading 4:	Key information: . . . .
Subheading 5:	Key information: . . . .

Step 2: Close your books/switch off the computer and write down everything you can remember about your chosen topic. The first time you do this it may not be a lot of information, but stick with it.

Step 3: Review your work, check for any errors and correct these areas.

Step 4: Repeat steps 2 and 3 two more times.

Step 5: Change topic. Mixing up the topics tested results in greater memory recall.

Step 6: Two hours later try to recall the information selected in steps 1 and 5.

Step 7: One day later try to recall the information selected in steps 1 and 5.

Final Thoughts

Sometimes we have a tendency to return to topics we know well. It makes us feel comfortable and confident to keep reviewing material we're confident about. But really you should be prioritising topics which you find trickier.

Try organising your topics from easiest to hardest. Which do you need to be spending more time on?

Easiest topics	**Hardest topics**
. . . .	. . . .
. . . .	. . . .
. . . .	. . . .
. . . .	. . . .
. . . .	. . . .
. . . .	. . . .

33. Vision Activity: What's Stopping You?

This thing in front of you. This issue. This obstacle – this frustrating, unfortunate, problematic, unexpected problem preventing you from doing what you want to do … What if it wasn't so bad? Holiday (2015), p. 1

Deciding what your goals are and making a plan can, quite often, be the easy bit. We usually set off with good intentions and then *boom*, we get hit with an obstacle or a number of obstacles that slow us down or in some cases stop us from following through on our goals. The first thing to remember is that this is completely normal. As Ryan Holiday says in the quote above, if you have a goal worth pursuing it's likely that there are going to be some obstacles on the route. So don't beat yourself up about it. Accept this as part of the journey and plan a way through – it might not be that bad!

Sometimes these obstacles can be completely out of our control – a sudden change of circumstances in our life such as illness or family problems, for example. However, we sometimes think that these obstacles are out of our control when in fact we might be able to do something about them. This activity is one to do if you find that you're not making the progress you hoped for. There are four steps and you'll probably need to spend about five minutes on each stage.

Step 1: Remind Yourself What the Goal Is

My goal is …

....

....

....

I know I will have achieved the goal when …

....

....

....

I should have the goal completed by …

....

Step 2: Circles of Control

For step 2 you need some sticky notes. Write down all the obstacles you can think of on separate notes, one for each obstacle. Just keep writing and think of as many obstacles as you can. The next step is to place them on the circles of control diagram below. This is how it works. Take each sticky note and first ask yourself, how much control do I have over this? Is it no control – there is nothing you can do about it (e.g. external factors such as ill health or family problems)? Or could you influence the obstacle – it might appear out of your control but there are some things that you could do to make it better? Finally, is this something that is in your control (e.g. you might not have been working hard enough but you know there aren't really any excuses for this)?

Circles of control

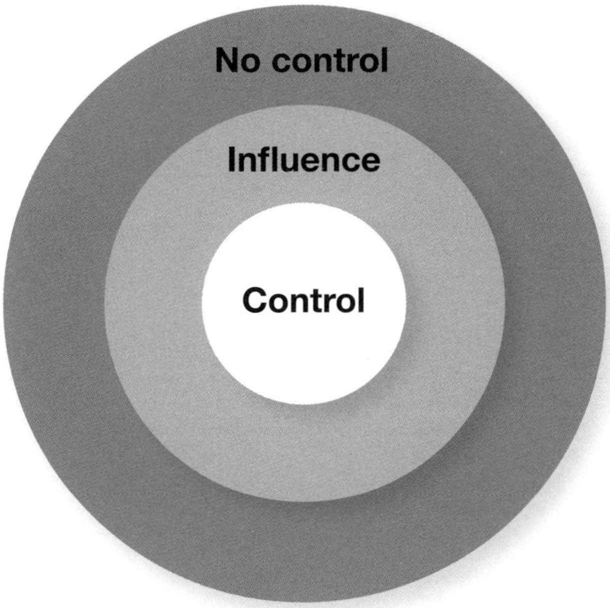

Source: Covey (1989), p. 82.

When you've decided where to place your sticky notes, it's sometimes useful to share your thoughts with another person, if you feel comfortable doing so. Sometimes we can believe we have no control when in fact we do. Getting a different perspective can sometimes help with this.

Step 3: Rate Your Obstacles

Next, take the sticky notes that you can influence or control and place them in the boxes below. You need to rate each obstacle on a continuum from 'stops me a bit' to 'stops me a lot' – think of it as a 1–10 scale.

If all of your notes are out of your control, you will need to seek some external support. Arrange to see your tutor or a mentor and describe the task you've done.

Stops me a bit **Stops me a lot**

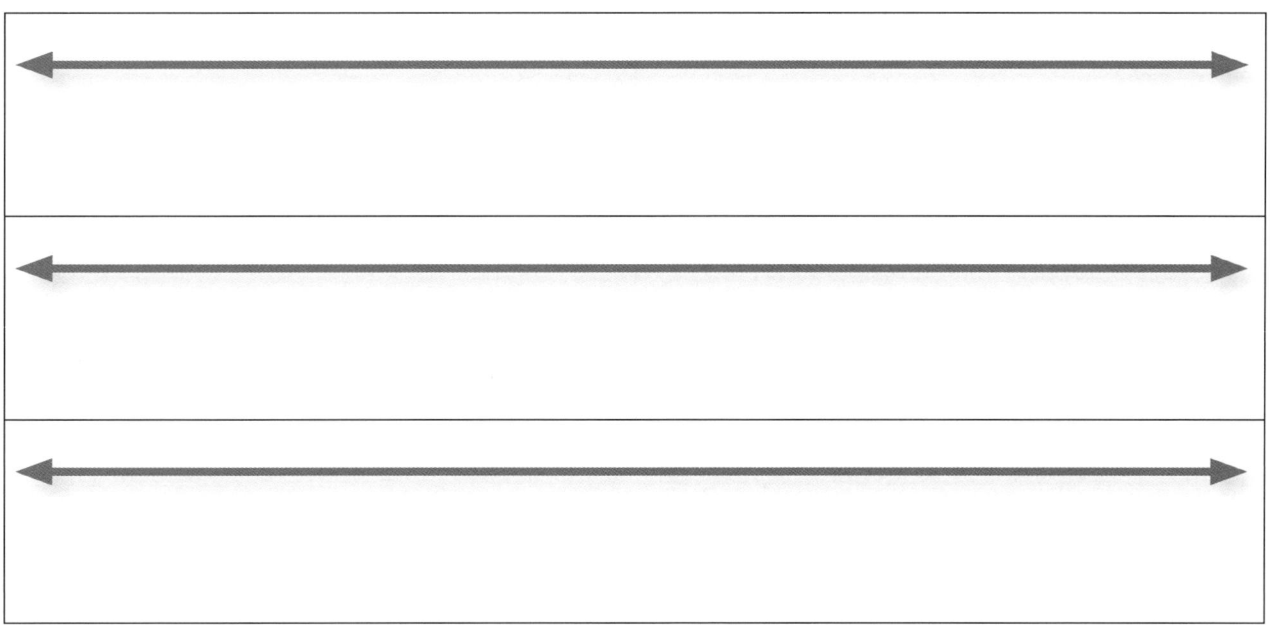

Stops me a bit **Stops me a lot**

Step 4: The Action Plan

Now it's time to take action. Take the three sticky notes that appear to be stopping you the most and place them in the boxes below. You then need to answer the three questions on each obstacle and decide what action you're going to take.

Obstacle	What could I do to overcome this obstacle?	What options haven't I considered?	What actions can I take?

Final Thoughts

For the first few times you use this tool it's best if you write the obstacles down. With enough practice you'll start to go through this process naturally in your mind. You'll find that with practice, rather than hitting a wall and suddenly stopping, you'll find a way around your obstacle.

April Activities

We've spoken to plenty of pupils who have told us they've fallen asleep whilst revising. And yet the same pupils wouldn't fall asleep in an exam. Why not? Because the exam is (i) hard and (ii) important. Often when we revise we make our work (i) easy and (ii) unimportant. Combine that with the choice to sit on a bed to do it, and you've got the perfect circumstances for falling asleep. This month's activities are designed to get you to think about how hard and important the work you set yourself is. If revision is intellectual combat, it should feel risky, challenging, slightly scary and weirdly exciting. If your revision is so dull it sends you to sleep, maybe you need to rethink what it is you do with your time – and where you work. Changing both could supercharge your exam preparation.

34. Practice Activity: Finding Flow

Many social scientists and academic researchers have become interested in the idea of 'flow'.

Flow is a high concentration, high performance state that we can all experience when we have the right task in front of us, the right space around us and the right balance of challenge and skill. You might well have reached what researchers call a 'flow state' before:

» If you've ever become so absorbed in a task that time seems to fly – perhaps writing, painting or playing sport.

» If you've ever sat down to work on something (it might not be schoolwork, maybe a personal project) and hours seem to have gone by in the blink of an eye.

» If you've been so focused that a two-hour exam might feel as though it's gone by in half an hour.

» If you've ever suddenly felt as though you're totally 'in the zone'. A sort of fully engaged, complete concentration on something fascinating and difficult.

People seem capable of amazing work when they're in flow. They make swifter progress, they learn quickly, they stretch and challenge themselves, and they operate at a higher level. They seem to expend more mental effort and often feel pretty exhausted afterwards.

Lots of social scientists have studied and written about how to reach flow states. Two observations have emerged:

1. There seems to be a connection between *flow* and *challenge*. You can't reach flow doing something so easy it doesn't require your full concentration.
2. There's a connection between *flow* and *your level of skill*. You can't reach flow trying to attempt something that's way beyond your current capabilities.

But get the right balance of challenge and skill, and you begin to approach flow. One social scientist has produced a kind of emotional map to show us where flow is. We've reproduced a version of it here. Think of a swimming pool with three lanes.

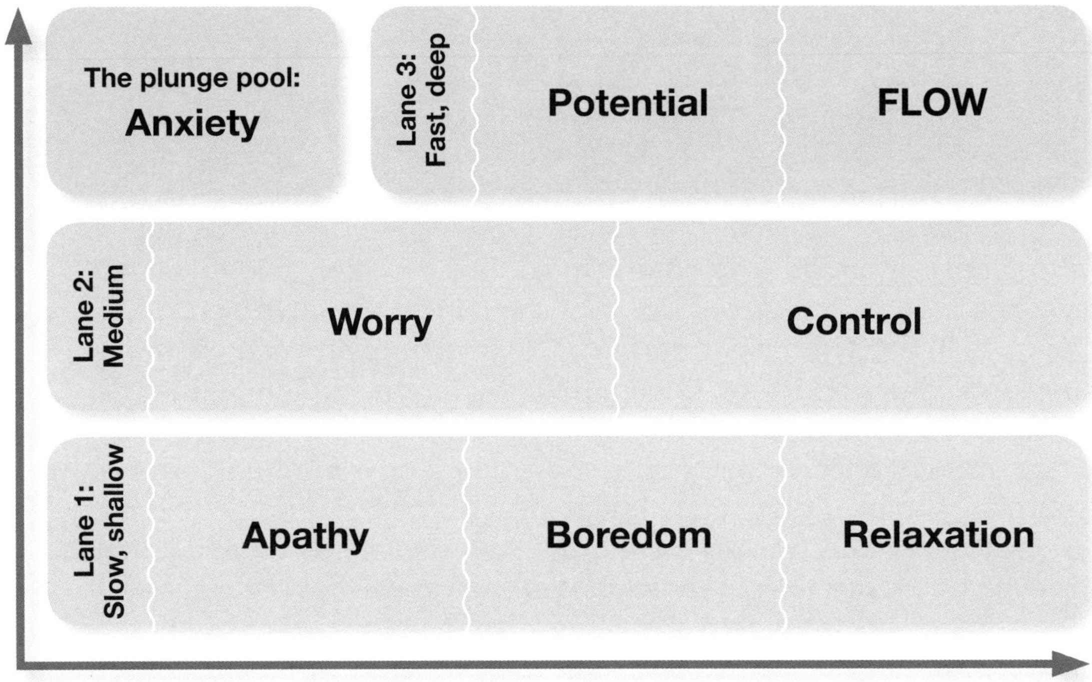

In lane 1 the water is warm. In other words, it's a nice, safe and comfortable place to be. The tasks here are low challenge and the work is easy. Even as your skill level increases, if you're in lane 1 you always feel relaxed.

In lane 2 the water is deeper and colder. It feels uncomfortable getting in if you're used to the warm water of lane 1. Swimmers move faster here – in other words, the work is harder. It often feels worrying, but stay long enough and you begin to feel in control.

In lane 3 the water is deep and cold. It's hard work here until you get used to it. Tasks are challenging and swimmers cut through the water quickly. Flow occurs in lane 3. There's no other way to get to it than by moving from lane 1, through lane 2 to lane 3.

The plunge pool – argh! Sometimes you try to move lanes too quickly, and end up losing your way and finding yourself in the plunge pool of anxiety. It's freezing in there! If you ever feel panic, if you feel overwhelmed or fearful, step back a little. Find a warmer, safer lane. Build your confidence there and then try to swap lanes again.

What Lane Are You In?

It could be that you're in different lanes for different subjects. So let's review your revision in just one subject.

Subject:

. . . .

How do you feel when you revise for this subject? Return to a memory from the last revision session you did. Now check that memory against the three lanes of the flow swimming pool. Your word might not be one of the words in the pool, but is it similar to one of them? Which lane do you think you're in at the moment? Record your thoughts here:

. . . .

. . . .

. . . .

Changing Lanes

Changing lanes is about increasing challenge. If you're interested in changing lanes, remember:

» You need to choose harder revision tasks to up your level of challenge and change lanes.

» This will start by feeling uncomfortable. Worry, stress or anxiety might be the emotions you begin to feel at first.

» But these feelings will disappear the longer you stay. Control or potential might be the states that replace it.

Let's finish by making a list of revision activities you could be doing. If they're easy and comfortable put them in lane 1. If they make you feel uncomfortable or slightly worried put them in lane 2. If the thought of them makes you feel dread and fear put them in lane 3.

Lane	Indicative emotions	Activity
1	Comfort, ease, confidence, boredom	....
2	Worry, discomfort, uncertainty	....
3	Dread, fear, stress	....

Next time you're feeling like progress is slow and you're comfortable and bored, you know it's time to change lanes. Choose an activity from a deeper, colder lane of the pool!

Final Thoughts

When you're in class, your teachers are often the ones pushing up the level of challenge. They might organise the lesson so that you're being forced to work in a less comfortable place. It's their job to do so!

It's natural sometimes to give ourselves a break when we're working alone. To ease the foot off the gas and do something simple.

So a good question to ask yourself is – *if we were revising/practising this in class, what kind of things would the teacher make us do?* Then do that, rather than return to those temptingly simple, shallow lane tasks.

35. Practice Activity: High Flow Spaces

The places we choose to work in often have a big impact on how effective our work is. Our environments can influence the quality of our concentration and focus in both positive and negative ways. An interesting study by two researchers at Reading University, Derek Clements-Croome and Li Baizhan (2000), found that UK office workers felt significantly less productive as their work environment became more crowded or cramped, as temperatures varied or as the quality of light diminished. A large majority of the subjects interviewed estimated they might get a 10% rise in productivity if their environment was better.

We've seen similar effects with thousands of pupils over twenty years of teaching. And, surprisingly, we've seen pupils who deliberately sit down to work in noisy, distracting locations so they can be disturbed. When we meet to talk about their lack of progress, they'll often tell us, 'Well, I tried to work, but I couldn't concentrate,' or 'I like working with lots of people around me.' Inevitably, when we check the quality of their work, they've expended lots of time but in fact got very little done.

What are your work environments like, and what link might they have to your levels of focus, concentration and flow? By figuring out where you work best, you can increase your levels of concentration – and get more quality work done in less time.

School Spaces

Try walking your school or college environment and mapping where your high concentration, high flow spaces might be. Visit study rooms, workspaces, your library and so on. Look out for:

» The levels of foreground and background noise in these rooms.

» The number of other people there.

» The behaviour of the other people there.

» The quality of the seating spaces (the tables, chairs and desks).

» The levels of light.

More than anything, try to capture a feeling – is this place calm and focused? If it is, you will be too.

Then make a list of places to go when you really need to get a job done – your high flow spaces – and places to avoid, even when the worst part of yourself might be persuading you to go there!

High flow spaces:	Positive qualities:
....	....
....	....
....	....
....	....
Low flow spaces:	**Negative qualities:**
....	....
....	....
....	....
....	....

Home Spaces

Now have a look at the space you have at home. It might be a shared space or a space you have to yourself. Try to examine it with fresh eyes. What is your desk like? What about the space around you? Is there a corner of your room which is a calm, quiet, high flow space?

....

....

If not, you need to make one. If you can't, you need to find a surrogate study space that is neither school nor home – an in-between space.

In-between Spaces

Think about your wider environment – the public spaces between school and home. Many pupils we've worked with over the years have found the perfect coffee shop or local library in which to revise or do independent work or prepare for tests. Others have worked on long bus or train journeys.

Draw up a list of places to investigate. Make sure they're easy to get to so that you can incorporate them into a new routine.

Possible in-between spaces:

1. ....
2. ....
3. ....
4. ....
5. ....
6. ....

Changing Spaces

Benedict Carey, in his book *How We Learn*, discusses some fascinating research about environment and memory. Research shows that changing the space in which you study increases your chances of remembering the material you've studied. Something about the freshness and variation in space makes the material more easily accessible in your memory. Swap high flow study spaces often and you may well remember more of what you've studied.

So, the more high flow study spaces you have at your disposal, the better you'll do!

Final Thoughts

A new, unfamiliar space often reminds us we're trying to work differently. Even a small change to your room at home works like a quick visual reminder that you're planning on practising harder!

Think about moving the position of your desk, pinning up some quotes, a timetable or some notes and reminders, moving your bed or your chest of drawers. All these small things will help reinforce the change you're making in the way you work.

36. Vision Activity: Now vs. Most

There's a famous quote, sometimes attributed to US president Abraham Lincoln, that goes like this: 'Discipline is choosing between what you want now, and what you want most.' It's a useful idea to think about because in many circumstances what we want now (to buy a pair of trainers, say) probably damages what we want most (to have enough money to go on holiday).

Many of us will find ourselves choosing what we want now over what we want most; it's human to sometimes make these choices. In fact, in some circumstances the 'now' choice (taking a break and forgetting our troubles for an evening) doesn't really damage the 'most' goal (getting great GCSE grades), so it's OK if we choose it. The problem comes if we *continually* prioritise 'now' over 'most' – if we do, we never end up reaching the goal we've set ourselves.

This exercise is an opportunity to look at the temptations you face now, to analyse how damaging they might be and to take stock of how often you choose them. It can help you to keep a check on your tendency to prioritise 'now' over 'most', not by denying yourself everything you want but by reaching a healthy balance.

Step 1

Begin in the right-hand column of the table below. Make a note here of *what you want most* out of your final GCSE year. It should include the grades you would be delighted to get but also the consequences of those grades: the pride and happiness others will feel, your sense of success and confidence, the courses you can go on to study as a result, the school or college you hope to attend, the friends you hope to be with and the personal qualities you want to have developed by the time you finish your courses.

Step 2

Now the left-hand column. Here, list everything you're tempted by on a daily basis: to skip homework, binge watch TV, avoid revision, spend time on social media – anything that pulls you away from your long-term goals on a daily or weekly basis.

What you want now	Scores	What you want most	Scores
....		....	
....		....	
....		....	
....		....	
....		....	
....		....	

Step 3

Now we're going to make a check of which 'now' activities are the most damaging. For each 'now' activity, give it two scores:

1. Give it a *regularity score*: 0 = you almost never do it, 1 = you sometimes do it, 2 = you often do it, 3 = you pretty much always end up doing it.

2. Give it a *damage score*: 0 = it does almost no damage to what you want most, 1 = it does a small amount of damage to what you want most, 2 = it does some damage to what you want most, 3 = it does a lot of damage to what you want most.

Now, times the two numbers together for each 'now' activity. Once you've done that, every activity in that column should have a score between 0 and 9.

Activities that score 4 or more present a challenge for you. You do them reasonably regularly and they have a negative effect. These are the ones you need to take a longer look at. Make a list of them here:

....

....

....

....

If your list is huge, don't worry – that's pretty normal. *Choose one or two as your priorities*. If you can begin by making a change to just one or two behaviours, you can work from there. If you feel your motivation dip, return to your lists and look at the right-hand column – remind yourself of what it is you really want.

Two behaviours to concentrate on eradicating:

....

....

Final Thoughts

One way to deal with problems you know will occur, is to make an if-then plan. Take the two behaviours above. You know for sure that these are the things you want now that will significantly damage the things you want most.

An if-then plan allows you to make a good decision about what to do when you're next tempted. Have a look at the table below, and see if you can make an if-then plan for your damaging behaviours:

If ...	**Then I will ...**
I end up chatting with mates at the bus station and they suggest staying out all afternoon ...	Tell them I have to get home because there's a family thing I can't miss, and catch the next bus. Plus I'll sit away from others so I can do some work.
If	Then ... .
If	Then ... .

37. Systems Activity: The Action Priority Matrix

As you move through the exam season, time will be limited and the pressure will be on. Inevitably, there are going to be moments when you have too much to do and not enough time to do it in. Here's where an action priority matrix can be super-useful. It's a real lifesaver because it allows you to differentiate between tasks according to how much impact they are going to have on your learning relative to the amount of energy you'll need to get them finished.

The grid looks like this:

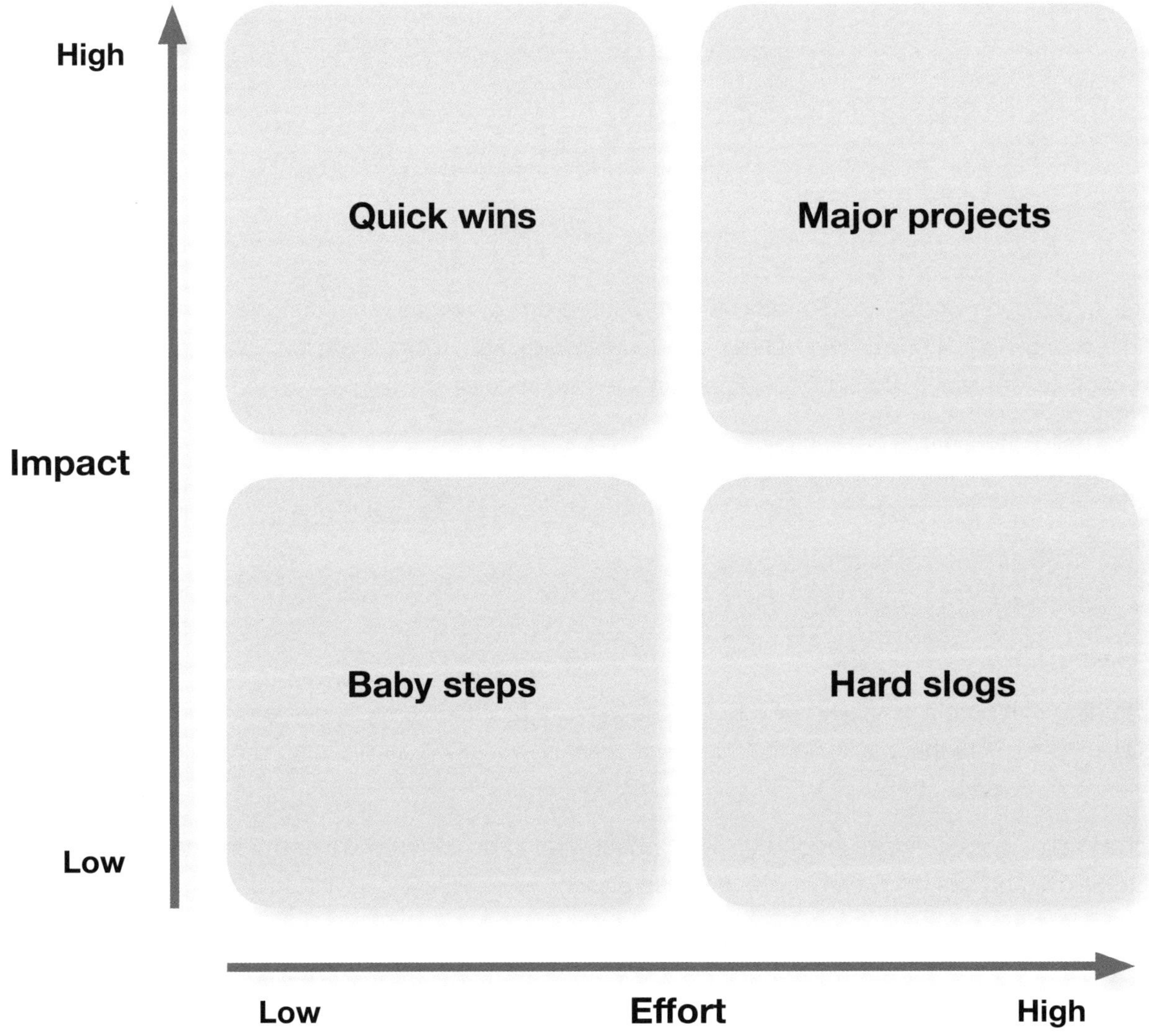

If you've got too much to do, try plotting all your possible actions on this grid. List everything you could be doing to prepare for the next two or three exams. Now weight them. First, consider how much energy they'll require. Energy means high concentration, focused time. If it's lots, put the action towards the right. If you could do it quickly and easily, put the action towards the left.

Second, consider the potential impact on your learning. If it's high – if you feel the action could really transform your knowledge or skills – put it up towards the top. If you think it will improve your learning a little, put it towards the bottom.

Once you've got all your possible options on the grid, have a look at which of the four quadrants the actions have fallen into and check out the following advice.

Quick Wins

These are gold. Get them done as a matter of urgency! They won't take long, and they could well transform your performance in a particular subject. If you've got an afternoon ahead of you (maybe even a full day, lucky you!), get these tasks done while you're feeling fresh and lively. Set a time limit for them – say to yourself, 'I'll do this task in thirty minutes' or 'I'll give myself an hour to get this finished.' Don't consider any other activities on the grid until you've bust through all of these.

Baby Steps

These tasks won't take much effort but neither will they have a massive impact. However, they could be good tasks to do if you're feeling foggy or lacking energy. They might not require total concentration, so if you need something to do just to get you into the rhythm of working, choose one or two. Similarly, if you've got a spare half an hour before lunch, or a spare twenty minutes before your bus, you could fire off one of these. Try doing one on the way into school for an exam – on a bus or train or in an environment that's not great for total concentration.

Major Projects

These are going to really boost your understanding and skill in a particular subject, but they're going to take a long period of high concentration to complete. Choose them if you can fulfil the following criteria:

» You have two to three hours where you won't be interrupted.

» You're committed to switching off all mobile devices for two to three hours, and you won't allow yourself to be distracted no matter what.

» You have access to a reasonably calm and quiet working environment.

If you can't fulfil these criteria, either change things so you can (call and cancel a meet-up, pull out of another commitment or switch location) or break the activities up. We've seen pupils have real success by taking a sledgehammer to a big project and bashing it into five or six smaller pieces. So instead of 'reread the complete chemistry textbook' (definitely a 'major project'!), pupils have broken the task down into 'reread chapter 1 and make notes' or 'reread sections 4 and 5, to pick out key ideas'. Suddenly, the big project becomes a set of smaller tasks that might end up in 'quick win' or 'baby steps'.

Hard Slogs

If you're really pushed for time, the chances are you'll end up not doing these; all your energies should be spent on getting your quick wins done, building up a load of activities in baby steps or breaking your big projects down into more manageable tasks.

Watch out, though – sometimes we might put an activity into 'hard slog' because we just don't want to do it. Could it be that you've subconsciously underestimated the impact the task could have on your learning? Only keep the task in 'hard slogs' if you're super-sure.

It's worth using this grid throughout May and June just to check in with yourself, to work out what you could be doing and to pick off those tasks which will have the highest impact.

Making Judgements

Imagine these were all tasks you could be doing with your time. Try adding them to the grid to help practise making judgements about effort and impact. Your answers might not be the same as others' – that's not a problem:

» Borrow a friend's notes and review that entire topic.

» Build a glossary of key terms with definitions.

» Ask three questions of my teacher, noting down the answers.

» Do a one hour reorganise of all my notes into topics.

» Ask for a textbook recommendation, then read the opening chapter, taking notes.

» Redo and resubmit that disastrous piece of work, asking for it to be marked again.

» Do a full, high-pressure two hour exam under timed conditions.

Final Thoughts

It's well worth reviewing the kind of work you do and thinking about the impact it has. Some pupils use the grid and realise they spend lots of time doing high effort low impact jobs. Others often figure out that they're doing lots of low effort low impact jobs over and over again.

Have you got a particular pattern of working? How might you improve it? Use the space below to record your thoughts and plans:

. . . .

. . . .

. . . .

. . . .

. . . .

38. Attitude Activity: Benefit Finding, aka The Rocky Road

Two psychologists, Robert Emmons and Michael McCullough (2003) at the University of Miami, asked this question: what if we reviewed stressful and difficult times and turned our attention to the lessons we learned from those negative experiences?

Three hundred pupils were asked to reflect on challenging periods of their lives: poor results, breaking up with partners, feeling insulted or offended, or being rejected from a particular course. Of the 300 subjects, 100 were asked to specifically focus on the lessons they had learned – the positive benefits that had eventually come from these challenges. It turned out that it was these pupils who coped better with their disasters and moved on from them. Emmons and McCullough found that positive benefits could flow from negative experiences.

David Collins, professor of coaching and performance at the University of Central Lancashire, has coached at the very top level, including being responsible for UK athletics at the Beijing Olympic Games. Collins, with his colleague Áine MacNamara, has done similar work to Emmons and McCullough. He's discovered that top athletes have travelled what he calls a 'rocky road'. This means that they've usually had their fair share of setbacks, failures and disappointments along the way. Often, we don't get to hear about these setbacks – we only hear about the successes!

The rocky road

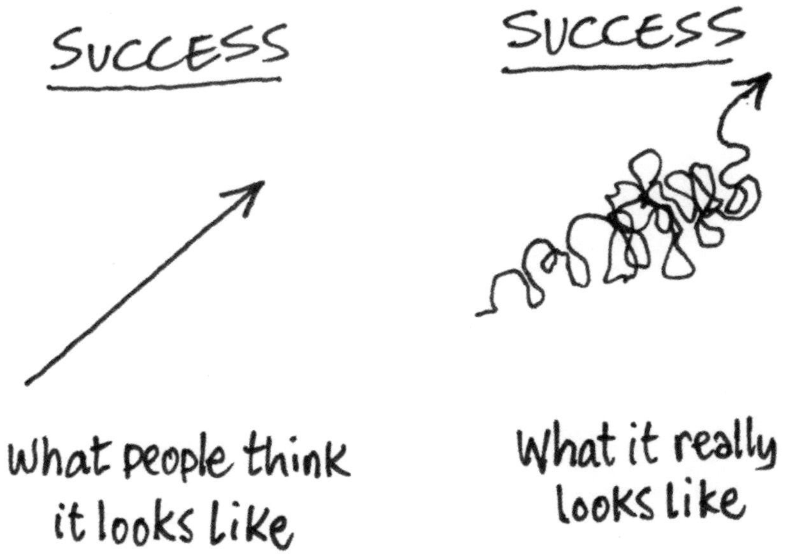

Professor Collins suggests that the rocky road might even be good for you as you will develop some useful skills along the way. The key thing is not to dwell on the setback and to bounce back.

Your exam period is going to bring challenges and difficulties, but you can use them as fuel. Think about a recent negative experience and look at the ten suggestions below. You don't have to address all of them but aim to make notes under at least five in the space provided overleaf.

1. A personal quality that has strengthened because of the experience.
2. A personal quality you didn't have at all that you've now begun to develop.
3. An increased appreciation of some part of your life as a result of the experience.
4. A valuable lesson you've extracted from the experience.
5. A realisation about life that you might not have ever considered before the experience.

6. An increased confidence about the way the world, or certain people, work because of what happened to you.
7. A skill you've developed or consolidated (e.g. thinking through problems, reflecting and understanding, communicating ideas, arguing confidently) because of the experience.
8. A relationship that has strengthened, perhaps with someone who helped or supported you through the experience or a stronger relationship with someone who hurt you.
9. A 'rule' you have extracted from the experience that you can now test in new situations.
10. A reassessment of certain priorities that might have happened because of the experience.

....

....

....

....

....

....

....

....

....

....

This piece of writing will remind you that we grow as a result of difficult times. Keep it somewhere close and refer to it when you need to!

Final Thoughts

We've found it really useful to normalise setbacks and problems by asking others about theirs. We've done it loads. It's such a relief to hear other people sharing their catastrophes!

You might ask a parent, an aunt or uncle, a friend or an older cousin. Teachers are often willing to tell you their stories too. A good prompt to start the conversation might be, 'Tell me the story of your biggest study disaster!'

Finish with, 'What did you learn from it?'

May Activities

This is it – you're going into battle. May is a time when you need to take care of yourself. Good sleep is important, good food is important, and space to reflect and calm yourself will work wonders too. There are only two activities this month. After all, your time will be spent in and out of the exam hall. But if you're feeling the pressure, try our First Aid Kit for three simple activities that always help. Like all well-being stuff, the activities can look a little weird, particularly if you're reading this in September. But set aside time to try them – they've worked extremely well for others. You could be the same.

39. Attitude Activity: The First Aid Kit – Three Exercises to Dissolve Stress

Box Breathing

(Time: 1–2 minutes)

For this exercise, you need to take four breaths, and as you do so, imagine building a box. Try this once or twice a day, and over a short period you'll begin to feel calmer.

Breath 3: In through the nose, four seconds, then hold for four seconds.

Breath 4: Out through the slightly open mouth across four seconds, then hold for four seconds when empty. Get back to your day!

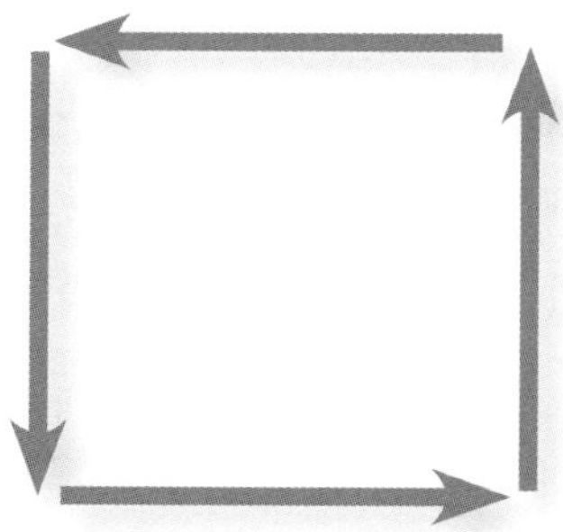

Breath 2: Out through the slightly open mouth across four seconds, then hold for four seconds when empty.

Breath 1: In through the nose, four seconds, then hold for four seconds.

Breath 1: Breathe in through the nose until the lungs are full and the chest is expanded. Take four seconds to fill your lungs. If you want a word in your head to help clear thoughts, the word can be 'right' as you imagine a pen travelling rightwards as it draws the bottom line of the box. Once you're full, hold the breath for four seconds.

Breath 2: Breathe out through the slightly open mouth. Take four seconds to totally empty your lungs. The word 'up' can be mentally repeated here if you need to, as you imagine a line being drawn up to make the right-hand side of the box. When you're totally empty, hold for four seconds.

Breath 3: Breathe in through the nose until the lungs are full and the chest is expanded. Take four seconds to fill your lungs. If you want a word in your head to help clear thoughts, the word can be 'left' as you imagine a pen travelling leftwards across the top line of the box. Once you're full, hold the breath for four seconds.

Breath 4: Breathe out through the slightly open mouth. Take four seconds to totally empty your lungs. The word 'down' can be mentally repeated here if you need to, as you imagine a line being drawn down to complete the box. When you're totally empty, hold for four seconds. You're done!

Deliberate Kindness

(Time: 30 seconds – 1 minute)

Suggested by a leader at Google, this deliberate kindness exercise takes very little time, but when repeated it has hugely positive effects. Because stress or anxiety is a focus on the self, activities like this work because they require you to place your focus on others.

Version 1

» Choose three people – parents, friends, peers, tutors or teachers, brothers, sisters or cousins.

» Give each of them ten seconds of your time, bringing them to mind, one at a time, as vividly as you can. Mentally say: 'I wish for this person to be happy.' Imagine them happy. Repeat the phrase mentally if you need to for ten seconds.

» Repeat for your three people. That's it.

Version 2

Try this in a public place – a study room, library, cafe, bus station, watching a crowd through a window somewhere.

» Cast your eyes over the crowds around you and choose three random people.

» Give each of them ten seconds of your time, one at a time, as vividly as you can. Mentally say: 'I wish for this person to be happy.' Imagine them happy. Repeat the phrase mentally if you need to for ten seconds.

» Do it for three people. You're done.

When repeated, this exercise trains your brain to spend just a little time focusing on others. Writer, teacher and entrepreneur Tim Ferriss says the following in his book *Tools of Titans* (2017, p. 159): 'I tend to do a single 3- to 5-minute session at night, thinking of three people I want to be happy, often two current friends and one old friend I haven't seen in years. A mere three days into doing this … I found myself wondering throughout the day "Why am I so happy?" … you easily get caught in the whirlpool of thinking about your "stuff". This loving-kindness drill takes the focus off you entirely – which, for me, immediately resolves at least 90% of the mental chatter.'

Concern vs. Control

(Time: 10 minutes)

This activity, adapted from Stephen Covey's excellent book *The 7 Habits of Highly Effective People* (1989), asks you to spend five minutes or so listing the things that are taking up your mental space and energy. Here's what you do:

1. Listen to your anxieties and worries (your 'mental chatter' as Tim Ferriss calls it) and write it all down – for example, 'worrying about the news', 'worrying about what questions might appear on my next exam', 'stressing about what people might think of my recent post on social media', 'thinking about ice cream'.
2. Put them all in one big circle, so they look as though they're all jostling around in your head. Now draw a second circle, off to the right or left, away from your head.
3. Next, review every item in the circle that looks like your head, crowded with crazy thoughts and issues, one at a time. For each item, ask yourself, 'What control do I have over this?'
4. If there's something you can do to control the outcome of the worry, it stays in the first circle (your head). Label this circle 'control'. If there's little or nothing you can do to control the outcome of the thought or worry, it leaves your head and goes to the second circle. This is going to be called 'concern' – the things you think about but have little or no influence over.

People who handle stress well minimise the stuff in the 'concern' circle. They practise forgetting about it. They spend their energy on the things in the 'control' circle and make plans. Finish the exercise by deciding *one simple thing* you could do to improve each of the issues/situations in your circle of control.

Final Thoughts

Feeling anxious or stressed about study is often a matter of perspective – about shifting your focus away from the self towards something else. That's why anything that makes you feel small or insignificant helps clear your head. If you're interested, here's two ways to do it:

The outdoors

We've spoken to pupils who have walked to the top of a hill near their house. From the top, the hugeness of the world makes them feel tiny. And that helps make them feel better. ('My problems seem stupid and small,' one pupil told us.) Another, looking out across the whole city, realised that there were others with much bigger troubles than they had.

The night sky

Another way to help realise the smallness of your life on this planet is to gaze at the star-filled sky. Again, all of a sudden, an issue with a GCSE test seems tiny in comparison to the vastness of the universe. And that can help you regain perspective.

40. Effort Activity: Pre-Making Decisions

Life is full of decisions. Each day we make thousands; estimates range between 3,000 for young children to something like 35,000 for adults. We all experience something called decision fatigue – a decrease in the quality of our decisions over a long period of decision making. (That's why those decisions we make at 10pm after a full day at school might not be our best!) It's partly because we often spend a lot of our decision making energy throughout the day on small material decisions – whether to buy this chocolate or that chocolate, what to eat for lunch and where to sit, how to spend a small amount of money, which bus to catch home and so on.

Often, our material decisions have taken up a lot of mental energy, leaving our behavioural decisions as unplanned reactions. So when a teacher challenges the quality of your homework, it feels unexpected and you might get angry even though you know you shouldn't. Or a friend asks you to skip an after-school class and you blurt out, 'Yes!' even though you know it's a bad idea.

This activity allows you to anticipate some of those decisions and to 'pre-make' them. Use the decision making energy you've got now to plan out responses to future events, and make decisions now that represent the best possible future you.

First, consider these questions and use the space below to answer them:

» What kind of person do you want to be?

» What qualities do you want to have?

» What's important to you?

» What do you want other people to say about you?

» What ideals do you want your strong, confident decisions to be based on?

....

....

....

....

....

....

....

....

....

....

....

Scribble down some notes and bear them in mind as you put yourself into some difficult scenarios. Some of them happen to everybody, and we've included them in the list. Others might be specific to your situation, so there's blank space lower down for you to add your own scenarios.

Scenario	Pre-made decision
You plan on doing some important research but your internet connection is down.	
You set aside some time to catch up on some crucial work but a friend arrives and wants to hang out and chat.	
It's one week until an important test and you know you've got a significant amount of revision to do.	
You're planning on working but a friend tries to persuade you not to.	
You have important tasks you want to get finished but there is something great on TV/social media/ the internet.	
A fellow pupil asks you to cheat on a test.	
A friend asks you to skip a class with them.	
A close friend suggests grades aren't that important – that revision is boring and school is worthless. They ask you to join them in quitting study and deliberately failing all exams.	

You can even add situations that help you to pre-decide even more crucial decisions. Think about how you would like the best version of you to respond if, for example, someone offers you drugs or you see a group of people mistreating someone.

You might not always make decisions that fill you with pride, but pre-making good decisions does make them more likely to happen!

Final Thoughts

One way to focus your mind on making good decisions is to recall times where you've made bad ones. Everyone can look back on a bad decision they've made, and the experience of reviewing it can help us figure out things to avoid in future.

Try recalling a bad decision. Focus on key details like – *Who was there? Where were you? What time of day was it? What was the exact point at which the poor decision was made? Why was the decision made that way?* Use the space below to record your thoughts:

. . . .

. . . .

. . . .

. . . .

. . . .

. . . .

. . . .

. . . .

Further Reading

Bull, S. (2006). *The Game Plan: Your Guide to Mental Toughness at Work* (Chichester: Capstone Publishing Limited).

Canfield, J. (2005). *The Success Principles: How to Get from Where You Are to Where You Want to Be* (London: HarperCollins).

Canfield, J., Hansen, M. V. and Kerberger, K. (1999). *Chicken Soup for the Teenage Soul: Stories of Life, Love and Learning* (London: Vermilion).

Carey, B. (2015). *How We Learn: Throw Out the Rule Book and Unlock Your Brain's Potential* (New York: Random House).

Cepeda, N. J., Vul, E., Rohrer, D., Wixted, J. T. and Pashler, H. (2008). Spacing effects in learning: a temporal ridgeline of optimal retention. *Psychological Science* 19: 1095–1102.

Cirillo, F. (2017). *The Pomodoro Technique: Do More and Have Fun with Time Management* (London: Ebury Publishing).

Clements-Croome, D. and Baizhan, L. (2000). Productivity and indoor environment. *Proceedings of Healthy Buildings 2000* 1: 629–634. Available at: https://www.researchgate.net/publication/237699305_Productivity_and_indoor_environment.

Collins, D. and MacNamara, A. (2012). The rocky road to the top: why talent needs trauma. *Sports Medicine* 42(11): 907–914.

Collins, J. (2001). *Good to Great* (London: Random House Business).

Csikszentmihalyi, M. (1997). *Finding Flow: The Psychology of Discovery and Invention* (New York: Harper Perennial).

Csikszentmihalyi, M. (2003). *Good Business: Leadership, Flow and the Making of Meaning* (New York: Penguin).

Duckworth, A. L. (2016). *Grit: The Power of Passion and Perseverance* (London: Penguin Random House).

Dweck, C. (2012). *Mindset: How You Can Fulfil Your Potential* (London: Constable & Robinson).

Dweck, C. (2017). *Mindset: Changing the Way You Think to Fulfil Your Potential* (London: Robinson).

Emmons, R. A. and McCullough, M. E. (2003). Counting blessings versus burdens: an experimental investigation of gratitude and subjective well-being in daily life. *Journal of Personality and Social Psychology* 84(2): 377–389.

Ferriss, T. (2017). *Tribe of Mentors: Short Life Advice from the Best in the World* (London: Vermilion).

Holiday, R. (2015). *The Obstacle is the Way: The Ancient Art of Turning Adversity to Advantage* (London: Profile Books).

Kleon, A. (2014) *Show Your Work! 10 Things Nobody Told You About Getting Discovered* (New York: Algonquin Books).

Landsberg, M. (2003). *Tao of Coaching: Boost Your Effectiveness at Work by Inspiring and Developing Those Around You* 2nd edn (London: Profile Books).

Martin, A. J. (2010). *Building Classroom Success: Eliminating Academic Fear and Failure* (London: Continuum).

Martin, A. J. (2011). Personal best (PB) approaches to academic development: implications for motivation and assessment. *Educational Practice and Theory* 33: 93–99.

McLeod, S. (2013). Kolb – learning styles. *Simply Psychology*. Available at: https://www.simplypsychology.org/learning-kolb.html.

Oettingen, G. (2014). *Rethinking Positive Thinking: Inside the New Science of Motivation* (New York: Penguin Random House).

Price, A. and Price, D. (2011). *Psychology of Success: A Practical Guide* (London: Icon Books).

Reiss, S. (2000). *Who Am I? The 16 Basic Desires That Motivate Our Actions and Define Our Personalities* (New York: Tarcher/Putnum).

Useful Websites

2. Vision Activity: Problem Not Job, aka The Personal Compass

The transcript from Derek Sivers' talk at the World Domination Summit is available at: https://sivers.org/wds.

4. Attitude Activity: Growth Mindset

Carol Dweck has developed a questionnaire that helps you to think about your mindset. This can be done here on her mindset website: http://mindsetonline.com/testyourmindset/step1.php.

If you'd like to learn more about growth mindsets, there are some fun videos here: https://ideas.classdojo.com/b/growth-mindset.

Also see: Dweck, C. (2014). The Power of Believing That You Can Improve [video]. *TED.com*. Available at: https://www.ted.com/talks/carol_dweck_the_power_of_believing_that_you_can_improve.

9. Vision Activity: Grit

J. K. Rowling's Harvard commencement speech describes the perseverance to continue her love of writing while experiencing professional rejection and doubt. You can watch it here: https://www.youtube.com/watch?v=wHGqp8lz36c.

You might also find it useful to watch Duckworth's famous TED Talk on grit at: https://www.ted.com/talks/angela_lee_duckworth_grit_the_power_of_passion_and_perseverance.

11. Systems Activity: Three Types of Attention

Think Productive (http://thinkproductive.co.uk).

16. Practice Activity: It's Time to Teach, aka CASTT

Cal Newport is a professor of computer science at Georgetown University, Washington, DC. He's written a few great books to help pupils achieve the best grades they can. It's worth taking a look at his website: www.calnewport.com.

18. Vision Activity: Success Leaves Clues

Rohn, J. (1981). Success Leaves Clues [video]. Available at: https://www.youtube.com/watch?v=lCXdTMB4qs8.

www.crownhouse.co.uk
ISBN 978-178583321-2
9 781785 833212
Education GCSE Study Guide